Understanding
The Godhead

*"My Personal Journey of
Discovery from Confusion to the
Truth, Without a Shadow of a
Doubt."*

by Joel Ridgeway

Published by Revealer Films

 **Revealer
Films.org**

Copies of this book can be obtained by going to
www.revealerfilms.org/Godhead.

**If you find this book a blessing, please consider donating to
our ministry, Revealer Films. This will help with the printing
of more books: www.revealerfilms.org/donate**

*All Bible verses taken from the Authorised King James Version,
unless otherwise stated.*

V1.4

Acknowledgments

First and foremost, I would like to thank my Heavenly Father for His longsuffering and patience with me as I stumbled along the path of life. Every time I muffed it, He was there to help me, and set me back on the right track. I also want to thank Him for giving us the Spirit of Prophecy, through the writings of Ellen G. White. Without these inspired books, my journey would be much more difficult.

Secondly, I would like to thank my parents for their dedication in raising me with strong principles and giving me a good foundation to build on.

I would also like to thank Robert, who was mentor in the early stages of my journey. If it was not for his insights and Biblical knowledge, I would not be where I am today. I also need to mention my good mate Emmanuel who's lateral thinking and keen perception has helped me express myself in a clearer manner.

I am most grateful for the late Pr Athal Tolhurst who critiqued this book years ago and wrote the forward. And to those who have spent hours proof-reading this book and giving me ideas, I would like to extend my sincere thanks.

Lastly, I want to thank my dear wife, Hannah, for her encouragement and support in embarking on the most challenging task of writing this book.

Table of Contents

Disclaimer

This book is not a personal attack on anyone. It is simply my own journey on this topic. I do use the word "trinitarian" and "anti-trinitarian" throughout this book, but only for the purpose of identification. I acknowledge that the word "trinity" is not used in the Bible and comes from Roman Catholic sources. I personally prefer to use the word "Godhead" or "Heavenly Trio" which are more Biblically sound.

Foreword

By Pr Athal Tolhurst

In the main, Anti-trinitarians, sometimes known as semi-Arians, are sincere in their acceptance of the divinity of Jesus Christ. However, unlike Trinitarians, they believe that God the Father produced Him by a process not clearly understood, and then bestowed divinity upon Him. Obviously this presupposes that Jesus did not exist from all eternity, and that He owes His existence to God the Father. In defence of this belief, they cite Biblical texts, beginning with those which refer to Jesus as the Son of God. They also claim that they alone are faithful to the beliefs, on this subject, of the pioneers of the Seventh-day Adventist Church.

The author of this book accepted the Anti-trinitarian teachings in his mid-teens. His approach to this subject is refreshing in that he simply outlines his own journey of discovery with openness and honesty. Since this book is written for Seventh-day Adventists, he feels free to quote extensively from the Bible and the writings of Ellen G. White.

I recommend a careful reading of chapter 1, for it lays down valuable principles of study when researching inspired writings. Once the reader understands these principles, the template is laid for the outline of Truth, not only regarding the Trinity, but for every Truth entrusted to mankind.

The author does not skirt around the difficult texts of Scripture. Rather he tenaciously compares them with the Truths revealed by the less difficult texts in his search for Biblical Truth. Because the Bible was not originally written in English, he occasionally searches out the original text in Hebrew for the Old Testament, and in Greek for the New Testament. This is a useful approach, for sometimes the Biblical writers' intended meanings become so much clearer, and what had appeared to be conflicts of meaning between texts of the Bible are resolved.

The author's research has been extensive as he unhurriedly wrestled with the differences between the anti-Trinitarian and the Trinitarian beliefs. This thorough research, particularly evident in the chapter entitled "Our Pioneers and the Doctrine of God", reveals that the Seventh-day Adventist Church today is not out of harmony with the Truth as discovered by its pioneers.

I recommend that every sincere Christian read this book carefully and prayerfully. As you travel along with the author, on his journey from Anti-trinitarianism to belief and acceptance, you will not only discover the beauty of this Truth, but you will thrill, as he did, at each discovery along the way.

Pr. Athal H. Tolhurst

Introduction

Do you believe in the Trinity? This one question has drawn the line in the sand for many Seventh-day Adventists. It certainly did for me. It has created two groups, in which are many diverse ideas and conflicting views. Depending on which person you ask, one group prides themselves because they believe in the Trinity or the Godhead, and the other group prides themselves in not believing in the Trinity. Still others are not sure what to be believe and just ignore the controversy, declaring that "silence is golden". Both sides claim to be following the Bible and writings of Ellen White. Both believe that they are walking in "Ancient Paths" blazed by our fathers, and are strong in the defense of truth. Yet, their ideas and philosophies are very different. When examined closely, both seem to have strong arguments in their favour. Here I stood, with two piles of evidence; both seemed to be equal in size, having their strong points and weak points. The result: confusion. Where does the truth really lie? This was my daily question. Someone is not telling the truth. They both cannot be right! I thought for a time that I knew the truth and was firm in it. Yet, as time lapsed, nagging problems kept arising in my mind that I could not put aside. My desire to be fully settled in the truth finally sent me back to the drawing board to reconsider this great question, Who is God? This book is the result of my search.

It is my prayer that this book will be a blessing to you and will help you in your search for the truth as it is in Jesus.

For identification purposes, I will call the two groups, "Trinitarianism" and "Anti-trinitarianism.

Trinitarianism generally teaches that God is made up of three distinct persons: the Father, the Son, and the Holy Spirit. All three are equal and have always existed. All have distinct roles in the plan of salvation.

Anti-trinitarianism generally teaches that the relationship that exists in the Godhead is on a more literal level. God the Father has always existed. He is the greatest of all. God then brought forth or begat a Son, and conferred complete Deity on Him, and the Son became the link between God and man. The Holy Spirit is not a separate being as taught by Trinitarians, but is the mind and character of God, spoken of as the third person.

The confused observer looks on and asks the question, "Who is right?" Perhaps the reason why this question has remained an enigma for so long is because we are asking the wrong questions. Maybe, instead of looking at both sides and trying to figure out who has the most evidence on their side, we need to go back to square one and ask, What is the truth? Somewhere, buried deep in this mountain of ideas, concepts and "evidence" is the truth. Sometimes it's like looking for a needle in a haystack; and it is little wonder that many miss the truth.

So, with one mighty sweep, let us push back all the confusion that has piled up over the centuries and go back to the beginning. Instead of going to man to find the answers, let us ask God Himself. God is the only one who can truly reveal who He really is. Tighten your seat belts for a journey through the inspired Word of God. It's going to be a wild ride at times, as we bump into the many ideas and interpretations out there: so hold on tight. Our journey will take us back to the very beginning of time, and beyond, to answer one of the most important questions of all time: Who is God?

As you proceed to read this book, I want to make one thing clear: you are not about to have one side of this debate crammed down your throat as being the truth. I am simply going to share with you what I have discovered in my study and where the Lord has led me. However, by the time you finish this book, the truth will hopefully be plain.

But I will also freely admit that I am way out of my depth here. This topic is so big, so vast, so incredible, that I don't even claim to have a basic understanding of who God is. All I can do is read what God tells us about Himself and believe it.

How to Use This Book

This book is not meant to be read the way you would read a novel. It requires careful thought and personal study. As you read through these chapters you will find a few helps that will aid you in your personal journey.

Throughout this book, I have placed dark grey boxes titled "Think about it!" and "Apply it to your life!" This is to help you think about the concepts presented and to encourage you to apply these things to your personal life. Doctrines are not any good to us unless they affect us personally.

You will see small numbers next to quotes and same words. These link with the footnote at the bottom on each page, giving you the reference or other important information.

In this book I will be quoting from many Bible verses and statements from the writings of Ellen White. It is not always practical to quote the full context of every verse. So I encourage you to look up the verses I am quoting, for yourself, and read the full context. If you have not heard of Ellen White, please go to www.whiteestate.org and here you will find out about the life and ministry of this amazing woman. Seventh-day Adventists (to whom this book is primary aimed) believe that her writings were inspired by God and that she was used by Him to guide the church.

A Challenge to the Reader

Dear reader, as you contemplate the truths that the Bible and Spirit of Prophecy have to offer, I entreat you to have an open and honest mind and prayerfully consider the facts I present. What you are about to read is not a cunningly devised thesis, with the sole intention of winning followers to my considered belief. What you will read is my personal experience and journey to seek to discover the real truth regarding the Godhead.

I was once an Anti-trinitarian. I firmly believed that Jesus was literally born of the Father in the ages of eternity. I was totally convinced that the Holy Spirit was not an individual, but the mind and personality of Christ. I thought I knew it all. I used to love to debate with people and slay them with my quick arguments and clever reasoning. Many people could not answer my arguments. Yet, as time progressed, God put me in various circumstances and brought various people into my life that made me become less arrogant in my views. I began to see problems with my understanding and verses that I could not harmonise.

I finally came to the point where I said, "Lord, take me back to the beginning". I went back to square one and studied the Bible and Ellen White with an open mind, and with the prayer, "Lord teach me the truth about You". Slowly, piece by piece, God put the puzzle together in my mind. He brought me into contact with people who gave me ideas and thoughts that I never had before. Bible texts and quotes that had been a mystery to me suddenly became plain! Wow, it was an amazing experience.

This book is the result of my search for answers. It is my hope that you will be able to grasp these truths for yourself. Take out the Bible and Ellen White's books and look up every quote I have used and read the context, and ask God to guide you.

This is my challenge to you today. Don't study with the intent of proving these things wrong. This is how all the false doctrines, which we face continually, have come into the church. Instead, with an open mind and prayerful heart, ask God to show you the truth. Lay aside your preconceived ideas.

If you discover something that I have missed or that is not correct according to the plain teachings of the Bible and the Spirit of Prophecy, please share it with me. I am always growing and learning in my experience. If there is anything that I am wrong about, the sooner I know it the better. So please, if I say something that is Biblically incorrect, don't go behind my back and endeavour to destroy my character in the eyes of others. Just e-mail me (joel@ revealerfilms.org) and I will be more than happy to look at any light you might have to share on this subject.

– The Author

Chapter 1

Laying the Foundation

Before we venture any further, we need to stop and consider that we are about to come close to the throne room of the great God of the universe; so we need to "take off our shoes", because we are standing on "Holy ground". I believe people too often rush into this topic and end up getting into trouble because they don't treat this subject with the reverence and awe that it deserves.

The main reason people come to wrong conclusions about God is because they rely on their own human reasoning to explain the Mighty God. The Bible says:

> *"...My thoughts are not your thoughts, neither are your ways my ways, saith the LORD. For as the heavens are higher than the earth, so are my ways higher than your ways, and my thoughts than your thoughts."* [1]

Ellen White echoes these thoughts:

> *"The most humbling lesson that man has to learn is the nothingness of human wisdom, and the folly of trying, by his own unaided efforts, to find out God. He may exert his intellectual powers to the utmost, he may have what the world calls a superior education, yet he may still be ignorant in God's eyes."* [2]

....
1   Isaiah 55:8,9
2   Selected Messages Vol. 1 p. 249

Charles Wesley once said *"You show me a worm that understands man, and I will show you a man that understands God."* Humanity trying to explain God is like a 4 year old trying to explain how a car works. Because the child and the Bible student really don't understand the object they are trying to explain, they must simplify it into something they do understand. This tendency to bring God down to our own level has plagued humanity ever since sin separated man from God. It has resulted in many horrible misrepresentations of God. The apostle Paul had it in his day. Referring to people who had this mentality he said:

"Because that, when they knew God, they glorified him not as God, neither were thankful; but became vain in their imaginations, and their foolish heart was darkened. Professing themselves to be wise, they became fools, And changed the glory of the incorruptible God into an image made like to corruptible man, and to birds, and to fourfooted beasts, and creeping things" [1]

Of ourselves we cannot hope to find out God. To try and do this is to end up making God like one of ourselves–"corruptible man." But God has revealed Himself to mankind through the Bible. The only way to understand God is to allow the Bible to explain God to us, without us adding to it what is not there. Rather then making up our own childish explanations that seem to make sense to us, we need to accept the simplified explanation that God has given us.

God has not revealed to us everything there is to know about Him. He has revealed only that which is important for us to understand in light of the Plan of Redemption. So don't be surprised when you find things about God that don't make sense to your human understanding.

....
1   Romans 1:21-23

Rules of Study

As we start out on our journey, we need some guidelines to help us on our way. We must first define some rules which we need to follow. The rules I am going to share with you, I did not make up. They are straight from inspiration. If you follow them, you are guaranteed to find the truth.

These rules apply to both the study of the Bible and the writings of Ellen White, which we will talk more about later.

Rule #1 – Pray before you open God's word

"Never should the Bible be studied without prayer. Before opening its pages, we should ask for the enlightenment of the Holy Spirit, and it will be given." [1]

How can you understand God's word without Him explaining it to us? The word of God in the hands of someone not guided by the Holy Spirit is a weapon of mass destruction that has caused untold damage to Christianity. It is from this source that have risen the plethora of false doctrines in the church. Why would we want more?

Rule #2 – We must have the right attitude

*"The spirit in which you come to the investigation of the Scriptures will determine the **character of the assistant at your side**. Angels from the world of light will be with those who in humility of heart seek for divine guidance. But if the Bible is opened with irreverence, with a feeling of self-sufficiency, if the heart is filled with prejudice, **Satan is beside you, and he will set the plain statements of God's word in a perverted light**."* [2]

....
1   Christian Education p. 59, Steps to Christ p. 91
2   Testimonies to Ministers p. 108

If we are studying to prove our opponent wrong and make ourselves look good, or have a preconceived idea in our minds, we **will** come up with wrong conclusions. We must have humility of heart when entering Bible study. Ellen White also says,

"When the word of God is opened without reverence and without prayer; when the thoughts and affections are not fixed upon God, or in harmony with His will, the mind is clouded with doubts; and **in the very study of the Bible, skepticism strengthens***. The enemy takes control of the thoughts, and* **he suggests interpretations that are not correct***. Whenever men are not in word and deed seeking to be in harmony with God, then, however learned they may be, they are liable to err in their understanding of Scripture, and it is not safe to trust to their explanations."* [1]

This is serious friends. If you are not seeking to be in harmony in word and deed with the scriptures, if you have pride and prejudice in your heart, Satan will be by your side directing your thoughts in the path of error.

Rule #3 – We must be right with God

Daniel tells us that *"none of the wicked shall understand; but the wise shall understand."* [2] The only way we can be "wise" and not "wicked" is if we are right with God. Isaiah says that *"your iniquities have separated between you and your God, and your sins have hid his face from you..."* [3] It is sin that separates us from God. If we are separated from God, how can we understand the truth? **If you have known sin in your life, please, lay this book down and make things right with God and man before you proceed.**

....
1   Steps to Christ p. 110
2   Daniel 12:10
3   Isaiah 59:2

Rule #4 – Take the Bible as it reads

"We are to take the Word of God as it reads, the words of Christ as He has spoken them." [1]

Very simply, what the Bible says is what it means. But this principal must be qualified. Because not every verse in the Bible can be taken as we might perceive it from a causal reading. Let me give you an example:

"And the devil that deceived them was cast into the lake of fire and brimstone, where the beast and the false prophet are, and shall be tormented day and night for ever and ever." [2]

If we take this verse on face value we must conclude that God punishes sinners forever and ever. But we know from other verses in scripture that this is not true. This is why our 5th rule of study is very important:

Rule #5 – The Bible is its own interpreter

"The Bible is its own interpreter. With beautiful simplicity one portion connects itself with the truth of another portion, until the whole Bible is blended in one harmonious whole. Light flashes forth from one text to illuminate some portion of the Word that has seemed more obscure." [3]

So we take the Bible as it reads, not adding or taking away from it, comparing scripture with scripture, allowing the Bible to explain itself. Most errors that exist in the Christian church can be corrected by this one rule.

....
1   Signs of the Times, August 18, 1887, par. 2, Lift Him Up p. 265
2   Revelation 20:10
3   Youths Instructor, June 30, 1898, par. 4, Our High Calling p. 207

Rule #6 – The Bible must be studied in context

"In order to sustain erroneous doctrines or unchristian prac-
tices, some will seize upon passages of Scripture separated
from the context, perhaps quoting half of a single verse as
proving their point, when the remaining portion would show
the meaning to be quite the opposite." [1]

This means before we make a conclusion about the meaning of
a verse, we must read the whole chapter to make sure our conclusion is in harmony with what the author was saying. We need
to consider the **internal context** and the **external context** of the
verse in question.

- **Internal context** is what is found in the verses surrounding the
  quote and also the whole chapter.
- **External context** is the historical setting in which the quote
  was written. Often understanding what was going on when the
  author wrote those words gives insight into what the author
  meant.
- We should also consider **word meanings**. Meanings of words
  change over time, so an old dictionary, and in the case of the
  Bible, which was written in a different language, a lexicon, can
  be very helpful.

This is very important when using the Bible to interpret itself. It is
often easy to find a verse which seems to be explaining another,
but if the contexts of both verses are totally different, we cannot use
it as a proof text. We are not inspired of God: how can we know if
the application is correct? Not following this rule can lead to grave
errors.

Rule #7 – A "multitude of counselors"

"There are a thousand temptations in disguise prepared for

1   Great Controversy p. 521

those who have the light of truth; and the only safety for any of us is in receiving no new doctrine, no new interpretation of the Scriptures, without first submitting it to brethren of experience. Lay it before them in a humble, teachable spirit, with earnest prayer; and if they see no light in it, yield to their judgment; for 'in the multitude of counselors there is safety.'" [1]

So if you do discover something new in the scriptures, don't instantly run and tell the world about it. Take it to persons of greater experience and humbly and prayerfully lay it before them. If they see no light in it, we are told to "yield to their judgment". That takes true humility!

The Key To Unlocking Inspiration

When crossing unfamiliar territory, it is very important to have a navigation tool to help you stay on track: something you can refer to, and to determine whether you are still headed in the right direction. A map and compass or GPS are good navigation tools for traveling on earth. Likewise, when we are traveling through the Word of God, we need spiritual navigation tools to keep us on track. It has always been said that the Bible is a map to guide us into the truth. This is of course correct. But can we take it a step further and say that we need a compass to help us use the map? A compass helps you reference yourself on the map. We also need a compass to help us navigate through the maze of concepts and ideas that are out there to find the truth. Otherwise we are destined to get lost. But we need not fear, God has given us such a guide. By the pen of inspiration Ellen White wrote:

"The central theme of the Bible, the theme about which every other in the whole book clusters, is the __redemption plan__, the restoration in the human soul of the image of

1   Testimonies to the Church Vol 5 p. 293

God. *From the first intimation of hope in the sentence pronounced in Eden to that last glorious promise of the Revelation, "They shall see His face; and His name shall be in their foreheads" (Revelation 22:4), the burden of every book and every passage of the Bible is the unfolding of this wondrous theme,--man's uplifting,--the power of God, "which giveth us the victory through our Lord Jesus Christ." 1 Corinthians 15:57.*

He who grasps this thought has before him an infinite field for study. He has the key that will unlock to him the whole treasure house of God's word." [1]

....
1   Education p. 126

APPLY IT TO YOUR LIFE!

Think about the last paragraph in this quote from Education p. 125:

"He who grasps this thought has before him an infinite field for study. He has the key that will unlock to him the whole treasure house of God's word." (Education p. 126)

This concept opens up a whole new gold mine of possibilities in your own personal Bible study. As you read a verse, think about what aspect of the Plan of Salvation is being revealed. The whole Bible can be renamed as *"The Instruction Guide for the Plan of Redemption"*. That is what it is for! Anything other than this is misusing it.

Imagine using the instruction manual for your car to try and understand how your washing machine works? You would get very confused, wouldn't you? This is what people do when they use the Bible to try and prove their own opinions. It is using the Bible in a way that it is not meant to be used. Next time you hear someone trying to prove something from the Bible, ask yourself, What has this got to do with God's plan to save me?

This is our key: the central theme, that every other theme in the Bible (including the Godhead) centres around is the redemption plan. So when we study this topic, or any other topic in the Bible, we must study it in relation to the plan of redemption. This is, after all, why the Bible was given to us in the first place—to show us the way of salvation. As Paul said to Timothy:

> *"And that from a child thou hast known the holy scriptures, which are able to make thee **wise unto salvation** through faith which is in Christ Jesus. All scripture is given by inspiration of God, and is profitable for doctrine, for reproof, for correction, for instruction in righteousness: That the man of God may be perfect, thoroughly furnished unto all good works."* [1]

The whole point of the Bible is to make us wise unto salvation, or in other words, to show us how God is going to save us from sin. When I discovered this truth, it really helped me to stay on track, and not get led away down some unimportant tangent. So as we continue our search through the Bible, let us keep this in mind. This will be the landmark we will keep in view.

Can We Trust the Writings of Ellen White?

God in His wisdom has given us the writings of Ellen White to aid us in our study of the Bible. Because our minds are so clouded after 6,000 plus years of sin, and because every wind of doctrine is now blowing; God saw that we needed a tool to help us understand the Bible.

As an anti-trinitarian, I was led to believe that not all of Sister White's writings could be trusted. Some words were changed here and there to suit the agenda of the church leaders of the time. But is this so? Can we safely trust *all* of the writings of Ellen White? This point I had to settle, before I could go any further. To my sur-

....
1   2 Timothy 3:15-17

prise, I found that these accusations are not new; they existed in Ellen White's day, and she herself has addressed them. She says;

"There are those who say, 'Someone manipulates her writings.' I acknowledge the charge. It is One who is mighty in counsel, One who presents before me the condition of things." [1]

"My copyists you have seen. They do not change my language. It stands as I write it. . . . I read over all that is copied, to see that everything is as it should be. I read all the book manuscript before it is sent to the printer. So you can see that my time must be fully occupied. Besides writing, I am called upon to speak to the different churches and to attend important meetings. I could not do this work unless the Lord helped me." [2]

"I have my work to do, to meet the misconceptions of those who suppose themselves able to say what is testimony from God and what is human production. If those who have done this work continue in this course, **satanic agencies will choose for them."** [3]

"I want to say, never repeat to another soul as long as you live the words that W. C. White manipulates my writings and changes them. This is just what the devil is trying to make all believe. W. C. White is true as steel to the cause of God, and no lie which is in circulation is of the truth." [4]

The truth is very plain. We can trust Ellen White because God has given her writings to us, and the way we have it is the way God has given it to us. Now I can hear someone say, "How do you know

....
1   Letter 52, 1906, p. 9; 1 Manuscript Release p. 30
2   Letter 61a, 1900; 3 Selected Messages p. 90
3   Letter 28, 1906, p. 2, To Brother George Amadon; 3 Selected Messages p. 70
4   Letter 143, 1906, p. 1, To Edson and Emma White; 4 Manuscript Release p. 240

that someone didn't forge that quote to cover themselves?" My response would be, do you think God will allow such corruption to go unexposed? You may be interested to know that attempts have been made to corrupt Ellen White's writings and God revealed it to her. Let me share with you the Fannie Bolton story.

The Fannie Bolton Story

Fannie was one of Ellen White's copyists who helped her write her manuscripts. Fannie had a few problems however, and Ellen White soon discovered that she was changing her writings to her own words. This is what Ellen White wrote about the matter:

"I told her again and again that I wanted not her words, but my words, and when I discovered words she had inserted of her own, in the place of the words in which I had expressed my ideas, I put my pen across it....

Fannie herself, notwithstanding the deception she was practicing, though she had, as she thought, deceived me for nearly one year, had the presumption to tell me that in her work of giving Bible readings, her words were inspired. She would tell how the ones she was talking with were wonderfully affected, and would turn pale. The strange part of the matter is that our own people are so ready to accept theatrical demonstrations as the inspiration of the Spirit of God. And I am more surprised, under the circumstances that they should encourage her to connect with sacred things.

She has urged, and begged, and cried, for me to take her back again into my service. But I said, "No, for you make false statements in regard to your preparing the articles for papers and books, which I deny. With all apparent sincerity and honesty you state to others and to me, that you think the Lord has inspired you to change the words I have traced, and substitute your own for them. I call this a strange fire of your own kindling." [1]

....
1   Manuscript Release #926 p. 60, 61

Ellen White had to break all connection with Fannie Bolton over this. She did much to hurt Ellen White's work, but God overruled.

If there was anyone else tampering with Ellen White's writings, God would have revealed it to her, just as He revealed what Fannie Bolton was doing. God will not allow His word to be corrupted.

We have no right to pick and choose what is inspired and what is not. If we do this, we start on a downhill spiral which leads to the eventual rejection of the Bible itself and everything else that we stand for. If we don't have something solid to plant our feet on, how can we be strong? Our only safe course is to accept the writings of Ellen White as one hundred per cent inspired. Otherwise, we must throw out Ellen White altogether. How can we know if other important truths that we read in Spirit of Prophecy are not manufactured by someone else?

I also discovered that almost all of Ellen White's "trinitarian" statements have been verified with her own hand writing, thus removing any possibility of forgery. See Appendix A for more.

Regarding compilations of Ellen White's writings put together after she died, we need to make sure we understand the context of the statements we are reading, before drawing any conclusions. The same applies to any study using the writings of Ellen White or even the Bible for that matter.

"The Bible and The Bible Only!"

Some people quoted to me Ellen White saying that "the Bible and the Bible only" is to be our standard, and they used that as a reason to lay aside Ellen White, because she did not agree with their ideas. But, I thought, would Ellen White discredit herself? So I went and read the context:

"But God will have a people upon the earth to maintain the

Bible, and the Bible only, as the standard of all doctrines and the basis of all reforms. The opinions of learned men, the deductions of science, the creeds or decisions of ecclesiastical councils, as numerous and discordant as are the churches which they represent, the voice of the majority--not one nor all of these should be regarded as evidence for or against any point of religious faith. Before accepting any doctrine or precept, we should demand a plain "Thus saith the Lord" in its support." [1]

I discovered that really, what she was saying is, a "thus saith the Lord" is needed, and not man's ideas and theories. Ellen White is inspired of God, so her writings are no less God's ideas than the Bible. There are no "degrees" of inspiration. Either she is inspired or she is not. I heard many people say that the Bible is before Ellen White. But I wondered, can God disagree with Himself? Is the prophet Daniel less inspired than the prophet Isaiah? Is not the same God speaking though them all? It is just like trying to compare Moses with Paul, saying that Paul is less inspired then Moses. Just because Ellen White came after the Bible was written does not mean her writings are less inspired. Inspiration is inspiration.

But, I also discovered that the Spirit of Prophecy is not a second Bible. It was given to us to point us to the Bible. Listen to what she herself says:

"The Lord has sent his people much instruction, line upon line, precept upon precept, here a little, and there a little. Little heed is given to the Bible, and the Lord has given a lesser light to lead men and women to the greater light." [2]

Ellen White's gift was given to act as a magnifying glass to make the pages of the Bible come alive to us. Its purpose is to motivate

1   Great Controversy p. 595
2   Review and Herald, January 20, 1903 par. 9

us to read our Bibles more. We need to be very careful when using Sister White's writings to prove our point. She had very strong words to people in her time who used her writings instead of the Bible;

"Lay Sister White right to one side: lay her to one side. Don't you never quote my words again as long as you live, until you can obey the Bible. When you take the Bible and make that your food, and your meat, and your drink, and make that the elements of your character, when you can do that you will know better how to receive some counsel from God. But here is the Word, the precious Word, exalted before you today. And don't you give a rap any more what "Sister White said"-- "Sister White said this," and "Sister White said that," and "Sister White said the other thing." But say, "Thus saith the Lord God of Israel," and then you do just what the Lord God of Israel does, and what he says." [1]

This is not to mean that we throw Ellen White's counsels away and only read the Bible. This is not what she meant! We need to understand that Ellen White's place is to point us to the Bible. So if the study of her writings does not make us dig deeper into the Bible, then we are misusing them. Our doctrines must be based on the Bible. Sister White can confirm the truth that we have and give some more detail, but she does not establish new truths.

What if I discover that Sister White does not agree with my application of Scripture? I should go back to the Bible and seek to discover where I went wrong, rather than disregarding Sister White. If she is inspired of God, what she has written is truth. So I need to take what is written in the Spirit of Prophecy as truth, even if it differs with my understanding of the Bible.

Throughout this book, I do quote extensively from the writings of

1   Spalding and Magan Collection p. 167

Sister White. This is because the Spirit of Prophecy has been used extensively by both sides of this debate to prove their points. So I must address these statements that are used so that the truth can be seen.

Let us therefore take seriously the inspired counsel that God has given, and not set it aside as of lesser importance or of no consequence.

Has the Bible been Changed?

There are some who will pick apart the Bible, saying that some verses are not inspired of God. But this is a serious error and leads to a slippery slope that ends in total shipwreck of faith in God's written word.

This quote from Ellen White is often used to justify setting aside some portions of scripture:

> *"I saw that God had **especially guarded the Bible**; yet when copies of it were few, learned men had in **some instances changed the words**, thinking that they were making it more plain, when in reality they were mystifying that which was plain, by causing it to lean to their established views, which were governed by tradition. But I saw that the Word of God, as a whole, is a perfect chain, one portion linking into and explaining another. **True seekers for truth need not err; for not only is the Word of God plain and simple in declaring the way of life, but the Holy Spirit is given as a guide in understanding the way to life therein revealed.**"* [1]

But we need to not ignore the first line in that Early Writings statement where she said that God has especially guarded the Bible. Thus we know that God has His hand over His word and has guard-

....
1   Early Writings p. 220

ed it from corruption. There is nothing in the Bible that would cause us to err from the truth if we study it using the methods of study outlined previously. We need to study the Word "as a whole" so that we will not get hung up by what may seem to us contradictions or mistranslations. No matter what the Devil may have tried to do in the past to blur the truth, God has made sure that it is clear to those who are willing to study His word using the methods of study that He Himself has outlined. And we need to always ask for the Holy Spirit to guide our minds before we study.

God has given us a treasure chest of knowledge at our finger tips today thanks to the advance of technology. Let us now delve into the Word of God and with the guidance of the Holy Spirit seek to discover how He has revealed Himself.

Chapter 2

The Nature of Christ

First and foremost in my mind was to discover the truth concerning the nature of Christ. Who is He? How long has He existed? What does His Sonship mean? Does all this really matter? What is the truth? With all these questions in my mind, I turned to the Word of God for answers.

Christ's Divine Nature

Studying through the Bible from Genesis to Revelation I found Jesus portrayed very clearly as God:

*"In the beginning was the Word, and the Word was with God, and **the Word was God.**"* [1]

*"(Christ) who is over all, **God** blessed forever. Amen."* [2]

*"For unto us a child is born, unto us a son is given: and the government shall be upon his shoulder: and his name shall be called Wonderful, Counselor, **The mighty God**, The everlasting Father, The Prince of Peace."* [3]

....

1   John 1:1
2   Romans 9:5
3   Isaiah 9:6

"And without controversy great is the mystery of godliness: **God was manifest in the flesh**, *justified in the Spirit, seen of angels, preached unto the Gentiles, believed on in the world, received up into glory."* [1]

"For this is good and acceptable in the sight of **God our Saviour**.*"* [2]

"But unto the Son he saith, Thy throne, **O God**, *is forever and ever: a scepter of righteousness is the scepter of thy kingdom."* [3]

"I am Alpha and Omega, the beginning and the ending, saith the Lord, which is, and which was, and which is to come, **the Almighty**.*"* [4]

So, without question, Jesus *is* God. But all Anti-trinitarians will usually agree with this statement. The real question in my mind was, what is "Divinity"? I need to know what this title of "God" really means. I discovered that there are two main attributes of God revealed in the Bible that give me a clear understanding of who God is. They are, His *creative power* and His *eternal existence*.

1. God as Creator

As I studied God's creative power, I found that the Bible portrays God as creative in three ways: Creator of everything, the Sustainer of all life, and His complete power over death. **Thus He is the Beginner of life, the Sustainer of life, and the Restorer of life.** What a beautiful concept!

---

1   1 Timothy 3:16
2   1 Timothy 2:3
3   Hebrews 1:8
4   Revelation 1:8

A. Creator of Everything

When we open the Bible to the beginning, the very first thing God wants us to know about Himself is the fact that He is our Creator. *"In the beginning **God created** the heaven and the earth."* [1] **It is a fact that the Bible writers understood that creating the world is a key attribute of God.** When seeking to establish the divinity of Christ, this is often the first place they went to. Here are a few examples:

> *"In the beginning was the Word, and the Word was with God, and the Word was God... All **things were made by him; and without him was not anything made that was made.**"* [2]

> *"God, who at sundry times and in divers manners spake in time past unto the fathers by the prophets, hath in these last days spoken unto us by his Son, whom he hath appointed heir of all things, by **whom also he made the worlds.**"* [3]

> *"...**by him were all things created,** that are in heaven, and that are in earth, visible and invisible, whether they be thrones, or dominions, or principalities, or powers: all things were **created by him, and for him....that in all things he might have the preeminence.**"* [4]

Clearly, creation of the world is a key attribute of God. This shows us that Christ is equal to the Father in creative power. He was the key player in creation. In fact the Bible makes it clear that all three persons in the Godhead were active in creation.

....
1   Genesis 1:1
2   John 1:1,3
3   Hebrews 1:1,2
4   Colossians 1:16,18

"And to make all men see what is the fellowship of the mystery, which from the beginning of the world hath been hid in God, who created all things by Jesus Christ" [1]

"Hath in these last days spoken unto us by his Son, whom he hath appointed heir of all things, by whom also he made the worlds." [2]

"And the earth was without form, and void; and darkness was upon the face of the deep. And the Spirit of God moved upon the face of the waters." [3]

But Christ's creative power is much more personal than that. This brings us to my next point:

B. The Sustainer of All Life

If Jesus is our Creator, then He is also our sustainer. He that has the power to create life, must also have the power to sustain life. What does the Bible have to say about the source of our life?

*"And he [Christ] is before all things, and **by him** all things **consist.**"* [4]

*"For unto us a child is born, unto us a son is given: and the government shall be upon his shoulder: and his name shall be called Wonderful, Counsellor, The mighty God, **The everlasting Father**, The Prince of Peace."* [5]

*"**I am the true vine**, and my Father is the husbandman. Every branch in me that beareth not fruit he taketh away:*

....
1   Ephesians 3:9
2   Hebrews 1:2
3   Genesis 1:2
4   Colossians 1:17
5   Isaiah 9:6

and every branch that beareth fruit, he purgeth it, that it may bring forth more fruit... Abide in me, and I in you. As the branch cannot bear fruit of itself, except it abide in the vine; no more can ye, except ye abide in me. I am the vine, ye are the branches: He that abideth in me, and I in him, the same bringeth forth much fruit: **for without me ye can do nothing.**" [1]

"All created things live by the will and power of God. **They are recipients of the life of the Son of God.** *However able and talented, however large their capacities, they are replenished with life from the Source of all life.* **He is the spring, the fountain, of life.** *Only He who alone hath immortality, dwelling in light and life, could say, "I have power to lay down My life, and I have power to take it again."* [2]

"From Jesus is our life **derived.** *In him is life that is* **original, —unborrowed, underived life.** *In him is the fountain of life. In us there is a streamlet from the fountain of life. Our life is something that we receive, something that the Giver takes back again to himself."* [3]

Wow! Christ is the original, unborrowed, underived fountain of life. We are streamlets, from Christ. This last quote was a clincher for me. It is very clear from inspiration that Christ is our sustainer.

If Christ is the source and sustainer of all life, the next question in my mind was:

Where did Christ's Life Come From?

As an Anti-trinitarian, I believed that Christ's life came from the Fa-

....
1   John 15:1-5
2   Bible Commentary Vol. 5 p. 1113, Manuscript 131, 1897
3   Review and Herald August 6, 1914 par. 1

ther. **Hence, the only true source of all life is the Father.** But what I had been finding in the inspiration had been challenging this idea. If Christ is the source and sustainer of life, then how could His life be generated at some point?

The last quote we read in the previous section really caught my eye. It clearly says that Christ's life is **original, unborrowed, and underived.** What does that really mean? The same phrase appears in the book Desire of Ages:

> *"Jesus declared, "I am the resurrection, and the life." In Christ is life, original, unborrowed, underived. "He that hath the Son hath life." 1 John 5:12. The divinity of Christ is the believer's assurance of eternal life. "He that believeth in Me," said Jesus, "though he were dead, yet shall he live: and whosoever liveth and believeth in Me shall never die. Believest thou this?" Christ here looks forward to the time of His second coming. Then the righteous dead shall be raised incorruptible, and the living righteous shall be translated to heaven without seeing death. The miracle which Christ was about to perform, in raising Lazarus from the dead, would represent the resurrection of all the righteous dead. By His word and His works He declared Himself the Author of the resurrection. He who Himself was soon to die upon the cross stood with the keys of death, a conqueror of the grave, and asserted His right and power to give eternal life"* [1]

According to inspiration, Jesus Christ has Divine life, which is described as follows:

Original: When something is "original" we say it is not a copy.

It does not come from something else. The life of Christ cannot be original if it came from the Father. The Father's life is original: He has always existed and always will. If the Father passed that life

----

1   Desire of Ages p. 530

onto Christ then it is not original.

Unborrowed: conveys the same idea as original. In fact, Webster's 1828 dictionary defines it as, *"Not borrowed; genuine; original; native; one's own."* [1] So the life that Christ possess is His own. It does not come from the Father.

Underived: means, *"Not derived; not borrowed; not received from a foreign source."* [2]

Ellen White has used three words that all mean the same thing. She has placed a **triple emphasis** on this one concept. This means that it is very important.

If she was trying to say that the life of Christ came from the Father, she did a very poor job of it. If Christ's life is truly original, unborrowed, and underived, then He has always had eternal life.

But, I argued, couldn't the Father have transferred His original, unborrowed, underived life to Christ? I turned to another of my favourite quotes:

> *"In him was life; and the life was the light of men" (John 1:4). It is not physical life that is here specified, but immortality, the life which is exclusively the property of God. The Word, who was with God, and who was God, had this life. Physical life is something which each individual receives. It is not eternal or immortal; for God, the Life-giver, takes it again. Man has no control over his life. But the life of Christ was unborrowed. No one can take this life from Him. "I lay it down of myself" (John 10:18), He said. **In Him was life, original, unborrowed, underived. This life is not inherent in man. He can possess it only through Christ.** He cannot earn it; it is given him as a free gift if he will believe*

---

1 Webster's 1828 Dictionary - "Unborrowed"
2 Ibid - "Underived"

in Christ as His personal Saviour. "This is life eternal, that they might know thee the only true God, and Jesus Christ, whom thou hast sent" (John 17:3). This is the open fountain of life for the world." [1]

Ellen White seems to be saying that we also can have life, original, unborrowed, underived through Christ. This has led many Anti-trin-itarians to say that Christ received His original, unborrowed, unde-rived life in a similar way.

But a careful reading of the whole paragraph shows us clearly that she is talking about two different types of life. One is the life of man, which he inherits through Christ. It is not original, unborrowed, un-derived when we have it. It is borrowed! Notice the second part of the paragraph:

"Physical life is something which each individual receives. It is not eternal or immortal; for God, the Life-giver, takes it again. **Man has no control over his life. But the life of Christ was unborrowed.** *No one can take this life from Him."* [1]

Ellen White is actually contrasting our life (unoriginal, borrowed, and derived from Christ), with Christ's life, that is original, unborrowed, underived. The difference is, Christ's life is unborrowed. Ours is borrowed. No one, not even God the Father, can take Christ's life away from Him. He chose to lay it down. This means that Christ's life did not come from the Father, otherwise the Father would be able to take it back again. Christ is the source of all life on earth. This brought me back around to the quote we read earlier:

"From Jesus is our life **derived***. In him is life that is* **origi-nal,—unborrowed, underived life***. In him is the fountain of life. In us there is a streamlet from the fountain of life. Our*

....
1   Selected Messages Vol. 1, p. 296

life is something that we receive, something that the Giver takes back again to himself." [1]

There it is: I sat in my chair spellbound. I thought, our life is derived, Jesus' life is underived. So it obviously isn't underived life when we have it! You can only have underived life if it is truly underived from anyone else.

The argument that God the Father transferred "original, unborrowed, underived life" onto Christ is completely without Biblical foundation. It is just an attempt to mystify a plain statement by inspiration.

C. Power Over Death

If God is our Creator and Sustainer, then He must have power over death. There is plenty of proof that God has power over death. This is not the main point that was burdening my mind. But I will give you one example anyway:

When Jesus first started His public ministry on earth, John the Baptist sent some of His disciples to Jesus with the question, *"Art thou he that should come, or do we look for another?"* [2] In other words, John wanted to know if Jesus was God in human flesh, the long-looked-for Messiah. Jesus answered: *"Go and show John again those things which ye do hear and see: The blind receive their sight, and the lame walk, the lepers are cleansed, and the deaf hear, the dead are raised up, and the poor have the gospel preached to them."* [3] Raising the dead was one of the proofs Jesus gave of His divinity.

The main point that was on my mind was this:

....
1   Review and Herald August 6, 1914 par. 1
2   Matthew 11:3
3   Verse 4 and 5

How Can Jesus, if He is God, Die?

If Jesus is truly 100% God, eternal and not subject to death, I asked, how can He die? Was it just a human body that died on Calvary? If it was just a human body that died, was it sufficient to pay the ransom for our sins?

After thinking and prayerfully studying the word of God, I came to the conclusion that I was asking an impossible question. God said it, so I need to believe it. Never mind the whys and wherefores. Faith believes the word of God without question. The Bible says that Jesus died. The Bible also says that Jesus is God. How? We don't really know. Therefore, I must just accept what the Word says without question.

God is very merciful however, and He has given us a few clues which strengthen our faith. Upon careful research, I discovered that the facts are laid down in black and white so we need not be confused over the matter.

"Was the human nature of the Son of Mary changed into the divine nature of the Son of God? No; the two natures were mysteriously blended in one person--the man Christ Jesus. In Him dwelt all the fullness of the Godhead bodily. When Christ was crucified, it was His human nature that died. **Deity did not sink and die; that would have been impossible.** *Christ, the sinless One, will save every son and daughter of Adam who accepts the salvation proffered them, consenting to become the children of God. The Saviour has purchased the fallen race with His own blood.*

*This is a **great mystery, a mystery that will not be fully, completely understood** in all its greatness until the translation of the redeemed shall take place. Then the power and greatness and efficacy of the gift of God to man will be understood.* **But the enemy is determined that this** *gift shall be so mystified that it will become as nothing-ness."* [1]

There it is, plainly written in black and white, "Deity did not die". That should be enough to settle the matter. If you are struggling with this question, please read the above statement again and again until you have made it yours. The Spirit of Prophecy tells us that this is a great mystery which we cannot fully understand until we get to heaven. So let us strive to be there and we will find out. As the prophet has said, our attempts to try and find explanations for this mystery have made it become "nothingness".

If it was impossible for Jesus' divine nature to die, that is irrefutable proof that Jesus is God, in the same way that the Father is God. **If Jesus' life had been somehow generated by the Father, then it would be possible for Him to die.** The Father could simply take back that life which He gave Christ in the beginning.

We are also clearly told that Jesus had the power to raise Himself from the dead.

*"I lay down My life, that I might take it again. No man taketh it from Me, but I lay it down of Myself. I have power to lay it down, and **I have power to take it again.**"* [2]

*"While as a member of the human family He was mortal, as **God He was the fountain of life for the world.** He could have **withstood the advances of death**, and refused to come under its dominion; but **voluntarily He laid down His life,** that He might bring life and immortality to light."* [3]

"Then answered the Jews and said unto him, What sign

....
1   Letter 280, 1904, 5 Bible Commentary p. 1113
2   John 10:17,18
3   Desire of Ages p. 484

shewest thou unto us, seeing that thou doest these things? Jesus answered and said unto them, Destroy this temple, and in three days **I will raise it up.** Then said the Jews, Forty and six years was this temple in building, and wilt thou rear it up in three days? But he spake of the **temple of his body.** When therefore he was risen from the dead, his disciples remembered that he had said this unto them; and they believed the scripture, and the word which Jesus had said." [1]

"When the voice of the angel was heard saying, "Thy Father calls thee," He who had said, "I lay down my life, that I might take it again," "Destroy this temple, and in three days I will raise it up," came forth from the grave **to life that was in Himself.** Deity did not die. Humanity died, but Christ now proclaims over the rent sepulchre of Joseph, "I am the resurrection, and the life." **In His divinity Christ possessed the power to break the bonds of death.** He declares that He had life in Himself to quicken whom He will."

"I am the resurrection, and the life." This language can be used only by the Deity. All created things live by the will and power of God. They are dependent recipients of the life of the Son of God. However able and talented, however large their capabilities, they are replenished with life from the Source of all life. **Only He who alone hath immortality, dwelling in light and life, could say, "I have power to lay down my life, and I have power to take it again."** All the human beings in our world take their life from Him. He is the spring, the fountain of life." [2]

Jesus gave up His life voluntarily. Death had no power over Him. It could not keep Him in the grave. When the time came for Christ to come forth from of the tomb, death could not hold Him.

....

1   John 2:18-22
2   Letter 280, 1904, 5 Bible Commentary p. 1113

It was Uriah Smith, one of the early Adventist Pioneers, that said, if only the human body of Christ died, and the spirit lived on, then we have a human sacrifice. He points out Isaiah 53:10 which says *"his soul"* was made *"an offering for sin."* [1] I totally agree. Notice that Ellen White in the quote we just read said "human nature" died. We know what the humanity is comprised of two things: body + spirit (or breath). So when Christ died, his human body and spirit both died. But notice a few sentences before Ellen White said that the human nature of Christ from Mary was not changed into divinity. They were blended in some mysterious way. The key word here is "mysterious" - it's not revealed to us. When Christ died, it was more then just a human body that died. In fact Ellen White tells us that:

*"The **spirit of Jesus slept in the tomb with His body**, and did not wing its way to heaven, there to maintain a separate existence, and to look down upon the mourning disciples embalming the body from which it had taken flight. **All that comprised the life and intelligence of Jesus remained with His body in the sepulcher**; and when He came forth it was as a whole being; **He did not have to summon His spirit from heaven. He had power to lay down His life and to take it up again.**"* [2]

So everything that comprised the life and intelligence of Jesus slept in the tomb. He laid down His divine-human life. We need to remember that Jesus was not just a human body with a divine spirit planted in it, that could take flight if the body was killed. The Divine and human were *"mysteriously blended in one person"*. [3] At any moment Jesus could have used His divine power to help His human body: in fact we read earlier that He could have resisted the inroads of death. But He **laid down** His life. God cannot be killed,

1   Uriah Smith, Looking Unto Jesus p. 23, quoting Isaiah 53:10
2   The Spirit of Prophecy Vol. 3 p. 203-204, Bible Commentary Vol. 5, p. 1150
3   Letter 280, 1904, 5 Bible Commentary p. 1113

but He can lay down His life. How this is possible will remain a mystery to us, for God is God and we are human.

At the same time, we need to realize that Christ really did take a massive risk by taking on humanity. Consider this statement:

> *Could Satan in the least particular have tempted Christ to sin, he would have bruised the Saviour's head. As it was, he could only touch His heel. Had the head of Christ been touched, the hope of the human race would have perished. Divine wrath would have come upon Christ as it came upon Adam.* **Christ and the church would have been without hope.** [1]

How can Christ be eternal God and yet take a risk like that? The answer is: we don't know. It is not revealed. As we read earlier in Bible Commentary Vol. p. 1113, the incarnation of Christ and His Divine-human nature are a mystery not revealed. So let us lay this one to rest for now. When we are in heaven we will then be able to understand many things that are beyond us now.

Didn't The Father Raise Jesus From The Dead?

There are in fact many Bible verses saying the Father raised Jesus from the dead. But we just read from Spirit of Prophecy that Jesus raised Himself from the dead. And Jesus Himself said regarding His life:

> *"No man taketh it from me, but I lay it down of myself. I have power to lay it down, and I have power to take it again. This commandment have I received of my Father."* [2]

....
1   Selected Messages Vol. 1 p. 256
2   John 10:18

It has been pointed out that the last sentence answers this by saying that the Father gave this power to Jesus. But this is twisting the statement to fit the anti-trinitarian mindset. We need to remember that in the incarnation, Jesus laid aside His omniscience (all knowledge). So that last sentence is simply saying that this statement that He has the power to raise Himself from the dead has been revealed to Him by the Father.

So who raised Jesus from the dead? I didn't have long to wonder: once again God's inspired messenger clears up the matter:

*"He who died for the sins of the world was to remain in the tomb for the allotted time. He was in that stony prison house as a **prisoner of divine justice**, and he was responsible to the Judge of the universe. He was bearing the sins of the world, and his **Father only could release him.***

*Christ had declared that he would be raised from the dead on the third day; and at the appointed time a mighty angel descended from heaven, parting the darkness from his track, and resting before the Saviour's tomb...The soldiers saw him removing the stone as he would a pebble, and heard him call, **Son of God, thy Father saith, Come forth.** They saw Jesus come from the grave as a mighty conqueror, and heard him proclaim, "I am the resurrection, and the life." The angel guards bowed low in adoration before the Redeemer as he came forth in majesty and glory, and welcomed him with songs of praise."* [1]

When the time was up, and Divine justice had been met, the Father could release Jesus from the tomb. Then Jesus came forth by His own power, declaring, "I am the resurrection and the life". The Father didn't have to give Jesus back His life so that He could be raised from the dead. Jesus came forth from the tomb by His own power, but He had to wait for the Father to call Him. So in this sense the Father did

1   Youth's Instructor, May 2, 1901 par. 9

raise Him up: The Father called Him and Jesus came forth of His own accord.

Consider this: if the Father raised Jesus from the dead, just like any other person that has been raised to life, how does that make Jesus conqueror over death? It really makes it of no effect. But if Jesus could actually raise Himself to life, that really does make Him conqueror over death.

2. Eternal & Self-existent

The second key attribute of God is that He is eternal. If God is creator of everything, it stands to reason that He must pre-exist everything else. My study revealed that the Bible is very clear in this regard:

*"The **eternal God** is thy refuge, and underneath are the **everlasting** arms: and he shall thrust out the enemy from before thee; and shall say, Destroy them."* [1]

*"Before the mountains were brought forth, or ever thou hadst formed the earth and the world, even from **everlasting to everlasting,** thou art God"* [2]

*"For the invisible things of him from the creation of the world are clearly seen, being understood by the things that are made, even his **eternal power** and Godhead; so that they are without excuse."* [3]

*"Now unto the **King eternal, immortal**, invisible, the only*

....
1   Deuteronomy 33:27
2   Psalms 90:2
3   Romans 1:20

wise God, be honour and glory for ever and ever. Amen." [1]

God is eternal. This is perhaps the most basic, fundamental characteristic that separates God from all other living beings. We cannot understand it, but we must accept it by faith. There was never a time when God was not.

In fact, I discovered that the Old Testament Hebrew word for God, "Yehôvâh",[2] comes from the root word "hâyâh", which simply means "to exist".

So the most foundational attribute which proves that God is God is the fact that He exists. To deny the eternal existence of God is to deny the existence of God Himself.

Jesus is also God. We know this from the clear word of scripture. So, without even going any further in the Bible, it stands to reason that Christ, being God, is also eternal, without beginning or ending. I dug into the scripture to test my hypothesis. What I found was astounding:

I found that the Hebrew words for God which mean "eternal existent" ("Jehovah" and "I AM") are used over and over to refer to Christ. In fact in the King James Version of the Bible, whenever you see the word "LORD" or "GOD" in capital letters, that is Jehovah, the Self-Existent One. We find these words clearly connected with Christ. Here's some examples:

*"And the **LORD** (the **Self-Existent One**) God formed man of the dust of the ground, and breathed into his nostrils the*

....

1   1 Timothy 1:17
2   Strong's Hebrew Dictionary: *"From* [hâyâh]; *the self Existent or eternal Jehovah"* Brown, Driver, & Briggs Hebrew Lexicon: *"Jehovah = 'the existing One'*

breath of life; and man became a living soul." [1]

Christ made all things, including mankind, according to John 1:3. So this is clearly a reference to Christ.

"For I am the **LORD** *(the* **Self-Existent One)** *thy God, the Holy One of Israel, thy* **Saviour***"* [2]

The word "Saviour" in this verse is "Yasha" which is Hebrew for "Jesus". We find this over and over in the Old Testament.

"I, even I, am the **LORD** *(the* **Self-Existent One)***; and beside me there is no* **saviour (Yasha)***."* [3]

"Tell ye, and bring them near; yea, let them take counsel together: who hath declared this from ancient time? who hath told it from that time? have not I the **LORD** *(the* **Self-Existent One)***? and there is no God else beside me; a just God and a Saviour* **(Yasha)***; there is none beside me."* [4]

"...I the **LORD** *(the* **Self-Existent One)** *am thy Saviour* **(Yasha)** *and thy Redeemer, the mighty One of Jacob."* [5]

"...I the **LORD** *(the* **Self-Existent One)** *am thy Saviour* **(Yasha)** *and thy Redeemer, the mighty One of Jacob."* [6]

"Yet I am the **LORD** *(the* **Self-Existent One)** *thy God from the land of Egypt, and thou shalt know no god but me: for there is no saviour* **(Yasha)** *beside me."* [7]

....

1   Genesis 2:7
2   Isaiah 43:3
3   Isaiah 43:11
4   Ibid 45:21
5   Ibid 49:26
6   Isaiah 60:16
7   Hosea 13:4

When God appeared to Moses in the burning bush (which inspiration tells us was actually Christ Himself [1]), Moses asked God what His name was, God said:

> *"...I AM THAT I AM: and he said, Thus shalt thou say unto the children of Israel, I AM hath sent me unto you. And God said moreover unto Moses, Thus shalt thou say unto the children of Israel, The **LORD** (the **Self-Existent One**) God of your fathers, the God of Abraham, the God of Isaac, and the God of Jacob, hath sent me unto you: this is my name for ever, and this is my memorial unto all generations. "* [2]

....

1   *"It was **Christ** who from the bush on Mount Horeb spoke to Moses saying, "I AM THAT I AM...."* Desire of Ages p. 23
2   Exodus 3:14, 15

THINK ABOUT IT!

As I compare what the Bible says about the Father and Christ, it has become clear to me that both are God in every sense of the word. There is no difference made between the two. In fact, if you carefully study all the references to God in the Old Testament and compare with what Spirit of Prophecy says, almost every reference is referring to Christ.

- Christ spoke with Abraham - Desire of Ages p. 290
- Christ appeared to Moses in the burning bush - Desire of Age p. 23
- Christ spoke the law from Sinai - Review & Herald Nov 28, 1893
- Christ lead Israel with the pillar of cloud in the wilderness - Christ's Object Lessons p. 287
- Christ glory dwelt in the Holy Shekinah above the mercy seat. - Christ's Object Lessons p. 288

Christ is the centre of the Bible. The Father's role does not really become prominent until Christ became incarnate.

Believe it or not, the word "I AM" is the Hebrew word "hâyâh", the root word of the name of God, which means "to exist". "I AM" means to exist. It signifies an eternal presence. God has always existed and always will exist. "I AM" means that God is eternal, without beginning or ending. And we see this name "I AM" directly linked to Jehovah, the Self-Existent One.

Several thousand years later, when Jesus stood on earth as a man, the Jews challenged His divinity with the question, *"Thou art not yet fifty years old, and hast thou seen Abraham?"* [1] Jesus replied, *"Verily, verily, I say unto you, Before Abraham was, I am."* [2]. The Jews reaction shows they fully understood what Jesus meant: *"Then took they up stones to cast at him".* [3] Jesus used the words that to the Jews meant the Self-Existent One, which equated to God alone, thus calling Himself God.

Commenting on this verse, Ellen White says:

"'Verily, verily, I say unto you, Before Abraham was, I am.' (John 8:53-58) Silence fell upon the vast assembly. The name of God, given to Moses to express the idea of the **eternal presence**, *had been claimed as His own by this Galilean Rabbi. He had announced Himself to be the* **self-existent One,** *He who had been promised to Israel, 'whose goings forth have been from of old, from the days of eternity.' Micah 5:2, margin."* [4]

Can inspiration say it any clearer? Without a shadow of a doubt, Jesus is eternal, without beginning or ending. If Jesus is truly God, then He must be without beginning, for one of the key attributes of God is His eternal presence.

....
1   John 8:57
2   Verse 58
3   Verse 59
4   Desire of Ages p. 469

A Very Impacting Statement...

I want to draw your attention to a verse we quoted in the last section, for it deserves careful consideration.

"Before the mountains were brought forth, or ever thou hadst formed the earth and the world, even from everlasting to everlasting, thou art God." [1]

This verse is talking about the Father. This verse shows His eternal existence and presence. From everlasting in the past and everlasting in the future: eternal, without beginning or ending. Ellen White confirms this truth. Referring to Daniel's vision of the throne room of God, she writes:

"Thus was presented to the prophet's vision the great and solemn day when the characters and the lives of men should pass in review before the Judge of all the earth, and to every man should be rendered "according to his works." The Ancient of days is God the Father. Says the psalmist, "Before the mountains were brought forth, or ever thou hadst formed the earth and the world, even from everlasting to everlasting, thou art God." (Psalm 90:2)" [2]

Yet I found that Ellen White also applies this verse to Christ:

"Before the mountains were brought forth, or ever thou hadst formed the earth and the world, even from everlasting to everlasting, thou art God" (Psalm 90:2). "The people which sat in darkness saw great light; and to them which sat in the region and shadow of death light is sprung up" (Matthew 4:16). Here the pre-existence of Christ and the purpose of His manifestation to our world are presented as

....
1   Psalms 90:2
2   Great Controversy p. 479

living beams of light from the eternal throne." [1]

I stopped and thought carefully about this connection for a while. Ellen White puts no difference between the eternal pre-existence of God the Father and Christ: "from everlasting to everlasting." This is clear proof that Jesus really is eternal.

Inspiration also says:

"God always has been. He is the great I AM. The psalmist declares, "Before the mountains were brought forth, or ever Thou hadst formed the earth and the world, even from everlasting to everlasting, Thou art God." (Psalms 90:2) He is the high and lofty One that inhabiteth eternity. "I am the Lord, I change not," He declares. With Him there is no variableness, neither shadow of turning. He is "the same yesterday, and today, and forever." (Hebrews 13:8) He is infinite and omnipresent. No words of ours can describe His greatness and majesty. [2]

We have just learnt that Jesus is the I AM. We have also read that Psalms 90:2 applies to Christ. Look up Hebrews 13:8. It also speaks of Christ. This then is clear proof that Christ is without beginning. Inspiration tells us "God has always been". Christ is God, so Christ has always been!

I came across the Great I AM again at the very end of the Bible. In the introduction to the book of Revelation 'grace and peace' is given from the heavenly trio:

"John to the seven churches which are in Asia: Grace be unto you, and peace, from him which is, and which was, and which is to come; and from the seven Spirits which are

....
1   Selected Messages Vol. 2, p. 248
2   Medical Ministry p. 92

before his throne; And from Jesus Christ, who is the faithful witness, and the first begotten of the dead, and the prince of the kings of the earth. Unto him that loved us, and washed us from our sins in his own blood..." [1]

So here we have:
- "Him which is, and which was, and which is to come" (The Father)
- "The Seven Spirits before His Throne" [2]
- "Jesus Christ"

I want to focus on the phrase, "Him which is, and which was, and which is to come". This is a very interesting sentence. The fascinating thing about it is that the whole English sentence, "which is, and which was, and which is to come", is translated from one particular Greek phase, "o᾿ ὤν o᾿ ἦν o᾿ ἐρχόμενος" (ho ōn ho ēn ho erchomenos). The Strong's dictionary defines it as follows:

"A phrase combining G3588 with the present participle and imperfect of G1510 and the present participle of G2064 by means of G2532; the one being and the one that was and the one coming, that is, the Eternal, as a divine epithet of Christ. (Each "and" (G2532) was ommited from the phrase because of limited space.): - which art (is, was), and (which) wast (is, was), and art (is) to come (shalt be)." [3]

This phase links directly with the "I AM" in John 8:58 and Exodus 3:14. It means "eternal presence" – the one who lived in the past, lives today in the present, and will live forever in future. This Greek phase is used four times in Revelation. Firstly in Revelation 1:4, and then in the following verses:

....
1   Revelation 1:4,5
2   Seven Spirits = "the eyes of Christ", or His omnipresence through the ministry of the Holy Spirit. See chapter 4 on the Holy Spirit.
3   Strong's Greek Dictionary, number G3801

"I am Alpha and Omega, the beginning and the ending, saith the Lord, which is, and which was, and which is to come, the Almighty." [1]

"And the four beasts had each of them six wings about him; and they were full of eyes within: and they rest not day and night, saying, Holy, holy, holy, Lord God Almighty, which was, and is, and is to come." [2]

"Saying, We give thee thanks, O Lord God Almighty, which art, and wast, and art to come; because thou hast taken to thee thy great power, and hast reigned." [3]

Two of these verses refer to the eternal presence of God the Father. But Revelation 1:8 refers to Christ. He is the Alpha and Omega, but He is also the Eternal One, and the Almighty.

Then we have Revelation 1:18, were Jesus says: *"I am he that liveth, and was dead; and, behold, I am alive for evermore, Amen; and have the keys of hell and of death."* [4] Commenting on this verse Ellen White says:

*"These are wonderfully solemn and significant statements. It was the Source of all mercy and pardon, peace and grace, the **self-existent, eternal, unchangeable One**, who visited His exiled servant on the isle that is called Patmos"* [5]

So the bottom line is that the Bible puts no difference between the existence of the Father and the existence of Christ. Both are eternal God, without beginning.

....
1   Revelation 1:8
2   Revelation 4:8
3   Revelation 11:17
4   Revelation 1:18
5   Manuscript 81, 1900, Bible Commentary Vol. 7, p. 955

Does the rest of Inspiration agree with this conclusion?

My next assignment was to ascertain whether or not the rest of inspiration agreed with my findings thus far. What I found was truly convincing:

*"From **all eternity** Christ was united with the Father, and when He took upon Himself human nature, He was still one with God. He is the link that unites God with humanity.* [1]

*"When Christ passed within the heavenly gates, He was enthroned amidst the adoration of the angels. As soon as this ceremony was completed, the Holy Spirit descended upon the disciples in rich currents, and Christ was indeed glorified, even with the glory which He had with the Father from **all eternity**."* [2]

*"The world was made by Him, "and without him was not anything made that was made" (John 1:3). If Christ made all things, He existed before all things. The words spoken in regard to this are so decisive that no one need be left in doubt. Christ was God essentially, and in the highest sense. He was with God from **all eternity**, God over all, blessed forevermore."* [3]

*"The terms of this oneness between God and man in the great covenant of redemption were arranged with Christ from **all eternity**."* [4]

"But while God's Word speaks of the humanity of Christ

1   Selected Messages Vol. 1, p. 228
2   Acts of the Apostles p. 38
3   Selected Messages Vol. 1, p. 247
4   Signs of the Times, August 24, 1891, par. 10, Amazing Grace p. 129

when upon this earth, it also speaks decidedly regarding His pre-existence. The Word existed as a divine being, even as the **eternal Son of God**, *in union and oneness*

THINK ABOUT IT!

Some people today affirm that Jesus was begotten or birthed by the Father far back in the ages of eternity. They claim that we cannot see beyond the invisible line of "eternity": So Christ was begotten in eternity, and therefore He is called "eternal". Yet here we have four statements saying that Christ has existed from ALL eternity–not just **some** of eternity, but **all**. All means all: without beginning.

"In speaking of His pre-existence, Christ carries the mind back through dateless ages. He assures us that there **_never was a time_** *when He was not in close fellowship with the eternal God. He to whose voice the Jews were then listening had been with God as one brought up with Him.* [1]

The context of this quote is one of the occasions when the Jews challenged Jesus' divinity. By making that statement, Ellen White is not trying to say that Jesus spent all His life communing with the Father. She is trying to draw our minds to "dateless ages"; eternity in other words. There was never a time that Jesus was not in close fellowship with the Father. That's what she said and that's what she means! It's that simple.

If Christ came into existence in eternity, then the above statement is not correct. If there was "never a time", there was NEVER A TIME! Some twist these words to make them fit their own faulty human reasoning. They will say, I can say of my father, 'there has never been a time when I did not love my Father', meaning that from the moment I came into existence, I loved my father. But is that really correct? What about before I was born? Did I love my father then? No of course not. This is just twisting words to make them fit their own preconceived opinion.

....
1   Signs of the Times, August 29, 1900 par. 15

*with His Father. **From everlasting** He was the Mediator of the covenant, the one in whom all nations of the earth, both Jews and Gentiles, if they accepted Him, were to be blessed. "The Word was with God, and the Word was God" (John 1:1). Before men or angels were created, the Word was with God, and was God."* [1]

*"Christ is the pre-existent, **self-existent Son of God**.... In speaking of his pre-existence, Christ carries the mind back through dateless ages. He assures us that there **never was a time** when He was not in close fellowship with the eternal God. He to whose voice the Jews were then listening had been with God as one brought up with Him."* [2]

When the Jews said to Jesus, *"Thou art not yet fifty years old, and hast Thou seen Abraham? Jesus said unto them, Verily, verily, I say unto you, Before Abraham was, I am."* [3] Commenting on this verse, Ellen White says:

*"Here Christ shows them that, although they might reckon His life to be less than fifty years, yet His divine life could not be reckoned by human computation. **The existence of Christ before His incarnation is not measured by figures.**"* [4]

I asked myself, if something cannot be measured with figures, what is another name for it? Infinity or without end!

In light of these very clear statements, we can see that Christ's Divinity is clearly linked to His eternal presence. Christ has always existed. This is one of the key attributes of God. To say Christ does not have this attribute is to deny His Divinity. Inspiration says,

....
1   1 Selected Messages p. 247
2   Evangelism 615, The Signs of the Times, August 29, 1900
3   John 8:57
4   Signs of the Times, May 3, 1899 par. 4

"The greatness of God cannot be measured or comprehended. And that doctrine that denies the absolute Godhead of Jesus Christ, denies also the Godhead of the Father; for no man knoweth the Son but the Father." [1]

The word "Godhead" means "Divinity". The Godhead is so closely united, that to deny the power or eternal existence of one, is to deny the power and eternal existence of all.

The Eternal Sonship of Christ

But if Jesus is completely and totally God, in every sense of the word, without beginning and without end, why is He called the only begotten Son of God, I wondered? Doesn't a son have to have a father and be born at some time? How can a son be the same age as his father? The concept baffled me for a time.

But then I realised, These are all human questions, based on a human understanding of humanity. The problem with using such reasoning is that we are trying to measure the **human** against the **Divine**. God says,

"For my thoughts are not your thoughts, neither are your ways my ways, saith the LORD. For as the heavens are higher than the earth, so are my ways higher than your ways, and my thoughts than your thoughts." [2]

"The mightiest created intelligence cannot grasp divinity. The principalities and powers of heaven are overwhelmed with the vastness of the theme of Christ's character and the mystery of the union of divinity and humanity. The most eloquent notes of cherubim and seraphim fail to describe him; but the angels of God delight to be in his presence." [3]

....
1   Signs of the Times, June 27, 1895 par. 3
2   Isaiah 55:8,9
3   Signs of the Times, June 27, 1895 par. 4

If angels with perfect minds cannot grasp Divinity, what hope do we have? All we can do is accept what is written in the Word and believe it, even though we might not fully understand it. God has given us all the evidence we need to understand the Plan of Salvation. Anything more than this is not needed and therefore God will not reveal it to us.

I must admit that accepting this concept was most difficult at first. To say that something you once thought you understood, is a mystery that you now don't really understand at all, is a hard pill to swallow. **But I have learnt that pride of opinion is one of the biggest hindrances to the advance of truth.** I must give up my right to think I understand some things.

But on the other hand, God doesn't expect us to rely completely on blind faith. Everything that is applicable to the plan of redemption about Himself He has revealed. But He reveals Himself in ways and words that we can understand. One such word is the word "begotten".

The "Begotten" Controversy

There is much controversy over the meaning of the word "begotten". This word is the main basis for the belief that Christ came into existence by the Father. Because the Bible and Spirit of Prophecy use this word to refer to Christ, many believe that this was proof that Jesus has a beginning.

But, I asked, what right do we have to make such a claim? Is our human understanding of words sufficient to explain the eternal God? Where is the Bible verse that says that Jesus has a beginning? I searched inspiration from beginning to end and found only a few vague references that can be interpreted either way (more on this later). **I realised that it is only assumed, because the "begotten" and "son" are used referring to Christ.** How do we know that these two words refer to the beginning of Jesus' life? Where is the "Thus said the Lord"?

This demanded further study, so I dived right into it. My study of inspiration's use of the word "begotten" in relation to Christ, show three applications of this word. All three of these applications see complete harmony throughout inspiration. Let me now take you for a tour down the hallways of inspiration and show you what I found.

1. The Eternal Plan of Redemption

We mentioned earlier that the way to understand the God-head is to look at it in relation to the plan of Salvation: Christ's Sonship is no exception. With this in mind, listen carefully to what Inspiration says:

> *"The Word existed as a divine being, even as the eternal Son of God, in union and oneness with his Father. **From everlasting he was the Mediator of the covenant,** the one in whom all nations of the earth, both Jews and Gentiles, if they accepted him, were to be blessed."* [1]

From everlasting Jesus has been the Mediator of the covenant. I ask, Mediator of what covenant? With whom was the covenant made? Man did not exist from all eternity, neither did the angels. Who was Christ mediating for before the creation of man, and the fall of Lucifer?

The Bible tells us that Christ is the *"Lamb slain from the foundation of the world"* [2] and that He *"was foreordained before the foundation of the world"* [3]. Spirit of prophecy tells us that:

....
1   Review and Herald, April 5, 1906 par. 5
2   Revelation 13:8
3   1 Peter 1:20

"Christ was appointed to the office of Mediator from the creation of God, set up from everlasting to be our substitute and surety." [1]

Therefore, Christ has had the title of Mediator from all eternity–as a surety of the work He would occupy once the plan of Salvation was put in effect. When man fell, Christ took on the office of Mediator, which was already in place, *"setup from everlasting."* First it was a promise or pledge, then it became reality when the time was right. This clearly shows us that Christ's name "Mediator" is a title that points to His work in the Plan of Salvation.

Could this principle also apply to Christ's title of "Son"? Question: was Christ called the Son of God before Bethlehem? The answer is yes. John 3:16 makes this very clear. But the only record we have in the Bible of Christ being born is at Bethlehem. This may come as a surprise to some people, but Christ has **always** been the Son of God. Here is the quote we read earlier with the addition of the next two paragraphs

*"The Word existed as a divine being, even as the **eternal Son of God,** in union and oneness with his Father. **From everlasting** he was the Mediator of the covenant, the one in whom all nations of the earth, both Jews and Gentiles, if they accepted him, were to be blessed. "The Word was with God, and the Word was God." Before men or angels were created, the Word was with God, and was God.*

*The world was made by him, "and without him was not anything made that was made." If Christ made all things, he existed before all things. The words spoken in regard to this are so decisive that no one need be left in doubt. Christ was God essentially, and in the highest sense. He was with **God from all eternity,** God over all, blessed forevermore.*

*The Lord Jesus Christ, **the divine Son of God, existed***

1   Review and Herald, April. 5, 1906

from eternity, a distinct person, yet one with the Father. He was the surpassing glory of heaven. He was the commander of the heavenly intelligences, and the adoring homage of the angels was received by him as his right." [1]

Notice that she calls Christ *"the eternal Son of God"*. This is very significant. Clearly, Christ has always been the Son of God. This seems impossible to our human reasoning: But once again we fall short when we try to fit God into our human mind set. **Just as Christ was called mediator from all eternity, He is also called the Son pointing to when he would become man's Substitute and Saviour.**

This helps to explain the following quote from Selected Messages:

"In His incarnation (Christ) gained in a new sense the title of the Son of God. Said the angel to Mary, "The power of the Highest shall overshadow thee: therefore also that holy thing which shall be born of thee shall be called the Son of God" (Luke 1:35). While the Son of a human being, He became the Son of God in a new sense. Thus He stood in our world--the Son of God, yet allied by birth to the human race. [2]

Christ has always been the Son of God. First He was the Son of God by promise, then He became the Son of God in reality. Thus He gained the title "Son of God" in a new sense.

Further to that, we are told that the plan of redemption has *always* been in existence. Notice the following Bible verses (note the words in brackets are based on the meaning of the original Greek words):

"Now to him that is of power to stablish you according to my

....
1   Review and Herald, April. 5, 1906
2   Selected Messages Vol. 1, p. 226

*gospel, and the preaching of Jesus Christ, according to the revelation of the mystery, which was kept secret since the world began (or **since times eternal**)"* [1]

*"But we speak the wisdom of God in a mystery, even the hidden wisdom, which God ordained before the world (or **eternal ages**) unto our glory:"* [2]

*"And to make all men see what is the fellowship of the mystery, which from the beginning of the world (or **eternal ages**) hath been hid in God, who created all things by Jesus Christ."* [3]

*"Even the mystery which hath been hid from ages (or **eternal ages**) and from generations, but now is made manifest to his saints"* [4]

The Spirit of Prophecy confirms this interpretation (notice Ellen White uses the alternative Greek rendering, "times eternal", when she quotes Romans 16:25).

*"But known unto God are all his works, and **from eternal ages** the covenant of grace (unmerited favor) existed in the mind of God. **It is called the everlasting covenant**; for the plan of salvation was not conceived after the fall of man, but it was that which was 'kept in silence through **times eternal**, but now is manifested and by the Scriptures of the prophets according to the commandment of the eternal God, is made known unto all the nations unto obedience of faith.' (Romans 16:25,26)*
       *The purpose and plan of grace existed **from all eterni-***

....
1   Romans 16:25
2   1 Corinthians 2:7
3   Ephesians 3:9
4   Colossians 1:26

ty. Before the foundation of the world it was according to the determinate counsel of God that man should be created and endowed with power to do the divine will. The fall of man, with all its consequences, was not hidden from the Omnipotent. Redemption was not an after-thought, a plan formulated after the fall of Adam, but an eternal purpose, suffered to be wrought out for the blessing, not only of this atom of a world, but for the good of all the worlds that God had created." [1]

*"The plan for our redemption was not an afterthought, a plan formulated after the fall of Adam. It was a revelation of **the mystery which hath been kept in silence through times eternal.**" Romans 16:25, R. V. It was an unfolding of the principles that **from eternal ages have been the foundation of God's throne**." [2]*

*"Nearly two thousand years ago, a voice of mysterious import was heard in heaven, from the throne of God, "Lo, I come." "Sacrifice and offering Thou wouldest not, but a body hast Thou prepared Me. . . . Lo, I come (in the volume of the Book it is written of Me,) to do Thy will, O God." Hebrews 10:5-7. In these words is announced the fulfillment of the **purpose that had been hidden from eternal ages.** Christ was about to visit our world, and to become incarnate." [3]*

*"The grace of Christ has made it possible that there be a close union between the receiver and the Giver. Those to whom God reveals by his Spirit the truths of his Word will be able to testify to an understanding of that mystery of godliness which **from eternal ages has been hid** in the Father and the Son." [4]*

....
1   Signs of the Times February 13, 1893, par. 3
2   Desire of Ages p. 22
3   Desire of Ages p. 23
4   Review and Herald, August 19, 1909 par. 7

*"The salvation of the human race has ever been the object of the councils of heaven. The covenant of mercy was made before the foundation of the world. It has **existed from all eternity, and is called the everlasting covenant.** <u>**So surely as there never was a time when God was not,**</u> **so surely there never was a moment when it was not the delight of the eternal mind to manifest His grace to humanity.**"* [1]

....
1   Signs of the Times, June 12, 1901 par. 7

APPLY IT TO YOUR LIFE!

"So surely as there never was a time when God was not, so surely there never was a moment when it was not the delight of the eternal mind to manifest His grace to humanity." (Signs of the Times, June 12, 1901 par. 7)

Wow! What a powerful statement! Doesn't that give you courage? God has a plan to save you and me from sin. He had that plan ready for us as long as He Himself has existed—without a beginning!

If Christ is without a beginning, then He has always had you and me in mind. The greatness of God is just so far beyond our human understanding. We cannot even begin to comprehend it!

"Redemption was not an after-thought, a plan formulated after the fall of Adam, but an eternal purpose..." (Signs of the Times February 13, 1893, par. 3)

The plan to save you and me was not just a quick emergency plan. It is the eternal purpose of the Godhead!

When temptation assails you, remember the power of God is waiting for you to use, in resisting temptation. This power is the eternal power of Jesus that knows no limit, only the limitations that we human beings place on it!

Can inspiration speak any clearer? The Plan of Salvation has always been in the mind of God, as an "eternal purpose". Just as surely as God has always existed, it has always existed. Before there was sin, there was a solution. In fact there **always** has been a solution, should sin arise. That solution was Christ becoming a man and dying for our sins.

Question: can there be an eternal plan of redemption, one that has always existed, without an eternal Saviour? Did God the Father form the plan of redemption without the Son and birth Him to fulfil this plan? What does that do to God the Father's motives? If the plan of redemption is eternal, then Christ, who is the centre of it, must also be eternal.

This helps us understand why Christ is called "the eternal Son of God". In the same way Christ has always been "the Saviour", even before sin existed, He is also "the Son of God" by the same token.

How much greater does the sacrifice of Christ appear if an eternal bond, far greater than the closest earthly father-son relationship, was broken for you and me! The Godhead was torn apart at the cross: or, as Ellen White puts it, there was a *"sundering of the divine powers"* [1]

In summary, we have learned that Christ is the Eternal Mediator, the Eternal Son and Eternal Savour.

This leads us into our second application of the word begotten: God's eternal love.

2. To Show the Love of God to Humanity

What was God's reason for using the word "only begotten Son" in reference to Christ, I wondered? Was He talking about a literal birth process, or is it something deeper? I decided to look up the words

....
1   Manuscript 93, 1899, Bible Commentary Vol. 7 p. 924

for myself: what I found surprised me.

The word "begotten" is used in reference to Christ ten times in the Bible. Of these, there is one Hebrew word and three Greek words which are translated "begotten." The meanings of the four original words are:

Hebrew #3205 – "A primitive root; to bear young; causatively to beget; medically to act as midwife; specifically to show lineage: - bear, beget, birth ([-day]), born, (make to) bring forth (children, young), bring up, calve, child, come, be delivered (of a child), time of delivery, gender, hatch, labour, (do the office of a) midwife, declare pedigrees, be the son of, (woman in, woman that) travail (-eth, -ing woman)."

Greek #1080 – "From a variation of G1085; to procreate (properly of the father, but by extension of the mother); figuratively to regenerate: - bear, beget, be born, bring forth, conceive, be delivered of, gender, make, spring."

Greek #3439 – "From G3441 and G1096; only born, that is, sole: - only (begotten, child)."

Greek #4416 – "From G4413 and the alternate of G5088; first born (usually as noun, literally or figuratively): - firstbegotten (-born)." [1]

Can these four words, I asked, be applied in the literal sense to Christ before the incarnation? Not in the sense that these words literally mean, because these words all refer to human reproduction. Now, as an anti-trinitarian I always believed that Jesus was begotten by a different process. Something like cell division, where the Father "brought forth" Christ out of Himself. This is what many anti-trinitarians believe today. But where does this concept come from? Certainly not from the word "begotten". In order to establish

....
1   Strong's Hebrew and Greek Dictionary

this concept, anti-trinitarians must use other verses to back this idea. Such as Proverbs 8:24,25, John 8:42 and John 16:28. We will address these verses in details in the next chapter.

This word can however, be applied, in a supernatural way, at the incarnation. But used before the incarnation of Christ, it is obvious that these words must be symbolic.

The Bible is full of illustrations to point us from earthly things, which we can understand, to heavenly things, which on their own, we cannot understand. *"For the invisible things of him from the creation of the world are clearly seen, being understood by the things that are made, even his eternal power and Godhead..."* [1] This verse clearly shows us that the Godhead is illustrated by things which are created on earth. These illustrations, though imperfect, give us a glimpse into the throne room of the Eternal.

For example: Christ is illustrated as a lamb in the Bible. *"He was oppressed, and he was afflicted, yet he opened not his mouth: he is brought as a lamb to the slaughter, and as a sheep before her shearers is dumb, so he openeth not his mouth."* [2] This is why, in the sanctuary service, the people had to bring a lamb as an offering for their sins. It pointed to Christ as the spotless lamb, quiet, gentle and submissive, who was to be cruelly killed for them. Christ is also called a Lion,[3] revealing another aspect of His character: one of kingly power and strength.

The husband and wife relation is also used to depict the love and tenderness that God has for His church. [4]

The names of the three persons of the Godhead also portray them in earthly terms, so we can understand them. God the Father is

1   Romans 1:20
2   Isaiah 53:7
3   *"Lion of the tribe of Juda"*, Revelation 5:5
4   See Romans 7:4 and Ephesians 5:22-32.

called a father, not because He is literally our father in an earthly sense, but because of His loving care for us, and how He sustains us moment by moment. The Holy Spirit is called the "Third Person of Godhead", yet is also call "A Spirit". (We will talk about the Holy Spirit in detail in a later chapter). This reveals to us the work of the Holy Spirit: not something that is seen, but something that can be felt like the wind.

Why then should we take the name of Son of God any differently? The Bible is consistent in its line of interpretation. It should be obvious that Jesus' Sonship means more than literal birth or generation by the Father. The Bible clearly tells us that Christ's *"goings forth have been from of old, from everlasting."* [1] As we have seen, the Spirit of Prophecy leaves no room for doubt in regards to Christ's eternal existence.

What does the name "Only Begotten Son of God" teach us? It tells us of the love of God.

> *"For God so loved the world, that he gave his only begotten Son, that whosoever believeth in him should not perish, but have everlasting life."* [2]

Now think about it: is it possible for an all powerful, creative God to have an "only child" in the literal sense? No, of course not! It is only humanity, with its limitations that has this problem. God is not trying to tell us that Christ is His only child.

What God is trying to tell us is that Christ contains everything that heaven has to offer. An only child is the sum of all the father and mother's effort. All that they have and ever will have is put into that one child. If that child dies, they have just lost everything. Their whole life is in that child. This is the lesson that God is trying to

....
1   Micah 5:2
2   John 3:16

teach us. Listen to how Ellen White so beautifully portrays this principle:

"The Lord could have cut off the sinner, and utterly destroyed him; but the more costly plan was chosen. In his great love He provides hope for the hopeless, giving his only begotten Son to bear the sins of the world. And since He has poured out all heaven in that one rich gift, He will withhold from man no needed aid that he may take the cup of salvation, and become an heir of God, and joint-heir with Christ. [1]

Our finite minds cannot understand the true depths of this great transaction. But this we know: we get a glimpse of the pain that heaven felt when Christ hung on that cross, when we look through the eyes of a parent. Imagine a parent witnessing his/her only child being abused and tortured, and being able to do nothing about it. This is just a small insight into what God felt.

How else could we understand the love of God? What other means could God have used to open our minds to the enormity of the price which was paid for us? Let us not allow our minds to get stuck in the literal, but on the wings of faith let us soar to the heights that God is calling us to. The more I learned, the more I became ashamed of my former ignorance! Thank you, Lord, for being so long suffering with me!

3. The Incarnation

The next principle I found follows on from the second. There are some clear verses that use "begotten" in reference to the incarnation of Christ. Hebrews chapter 1 is a good example. Let us study some of this chapter. Below is Hebrews 1:1-6. I will be commenting on certain verses as we go:

---

1   Bible Echo, March 15, 1893 par. 3

1:1 "God who at sundry times and in divers manners spake in time past unto the fathers by the prophets,
1:2   Hath in these last days spoken unto us by his Son, whom he hath appointed heir of all things, by whom also he made the worlds;"

This sets the theme for the chapter. We are talking about Christ and how God reveals Himself to us. First it was through human mediums, but now that Christ has taken on humanity, the communication goes through Him. Then Paul goes on to describe Christ and His incarnation:

1:3 "Who being the brightness of his glory, and the express

APPLY IT TO YOUR LIFE!

If the Father and Christ have been one in their Divine relationship from eternity, this puts their relationship on a much deeper level than any earthly father-son relationship. Their eternal bond has always been. It had never been broken, until Jesus took sin upon Himself. The Godhead was torn apart at Calvary! Such thoughts are too big for the human mind to grasp. How can Divine beings suffer so much pain?

The pain and the loss of blood from His wounds did not kill Christ. It was the eternal bond with the Godhead which was torn apart at Calvary that killed the Son of God.

This makes the sacrifice of Jesus so much greater and far beyond our comprehension than a human–derived theory, that Christ, a God–originated being, came and died for us. It was the Eternal Almighty God Himself that stooped to take on humanity and become one with us.

The theory that Jesus was brought into existence by the Father is a humanistic way of explaining something far too great and wonderful for our comprehension.

image of his person, and upholding all things by the word of his power, when he had by himself purged our sins, sat down on the right hand of the Majesty on high;"

This verse takes the whole plan of redemption in one sweep. From the start, being equal with God, and upholding the world with His own power, he stooped low to raise up humanity and then sat on the right hand of God.

1:4 Being made so much better than the angels, as he hath by inheritance obtained a more excellent name than they.

What made Jesus so much better than the angels? Why did he have a more excellent name than they? By **inheritance**. Keep this in mind, as we will come back to it. Read the next verse:

*1:5 For unto which of the angels said he at any time, Thou art my son, **this day have I begotten thee?** And again, I will be to him a **Father**, and he shall be to me a **Son**?*

Alright, stop right here. What is the setting of the last few verses? Christ's mission to save the world. Remember what Ellen White said about the Bible? **The central theme is the redemption plan.** So from that, and the evidence we have looked at earlier, we can conclude that this has something to do with the incarnation. But to be sure, let's read the verse where this is taken from. Paul was quoting from Psalm 2:7. In fact Hebrews 1 follows the same pattern as Psalms 2:

2:1 Why do the heathen rage, and the people imagine a vain thing?
2:2 The kings of the earth set themselves, and the rulers take counsel together, against the LORD, and against his anointed, saying,
2:3 Let us break their bands asunder, and cast away their cords from us.

When did the heathen rage and set themselves up against Christ? When he was begotten in eternity past? I don't think so. The only time recorded in the Bible when sinners where able to get their hands on Christ, was at Calvary.

> *2:4 He that sitteth in the heavens shall laugh: the Lord shall have them in derision.*
> *2:5 Then shall he speak unto them in his wrath, and vex them in his sore displeasure.*

When did God discomfort the people who tried to keep Christ in the tomb? It is written plain as day in Spirit of Prophecy Vol 3:

> *"How must God and his holy angels have looked upon all those preparations to guard the body of the world's Redeemer! How weak and foolish must those efforts have seemed! The words of the psalmist picture this scene: "**Why do the heathen rage, and the people imagine a vain thing? The kings of the earth set themselves, and the rulers take counsel together against the Lord, and against his Anointed, saying, Let us break their bands asunder, and cast away their cords from us. He that sitteth in the heavens shall laugh; the Lord shall have them in derision.**" Roman guards and Roman arms were powerless to confine the Lord of life within the narrow inclosure of the sepulcher. Christ had declared that he had power to lay down his life and to take it up again. The hour of his victory was near."* [1]

As we read on in Psalms two, we will discover that Hebrews chapter one follows a similar line of thought. I will now put them side by side;

---

1   Spirit of Prophecy Vol. 3 p. 179

Psalms 2	Hebrews 1
2:6 "Yet have I **set my king upon my holy hill of Zion.**"	1:3 "...when he had by himself purged our sins, **sat down on the right hand of the Majesty on high;**"
2:7 "I will declare the decree: the LORD hath said unto me, **Thou art my Son; this day have I begotten thee.**"	1:5 "For unto which of the angels said he at any time, **Thou art my son, this day have I begotten thee?**"
2:8 "Ask of me, and I give thee the heathen for thine **inheritance**, and the uttermost parts of the earth for thy possession	1:4 "Being made so much better than the angels, as he hath by **inheritance** obtained a more excellent name than they."

Can you see that both these chapters are talking about the same event? Remember what gave Jesus a greater name than the angels in Hebrews 1:4? His **inheritance**. What was the inheritance given to Christ? The heathen being converted by His love and by His death on the cross. This is what exalted Him in the eyes of the angels.

The verses in Psalms 2 are a prophecy of Christ's resurrection from the dead. Therefore, Hebrews 1 is also talking about the same event and is not referring to a time when Christ was brought into existence by the Father. "Begotten" in this context is referring to the incarnation. The time when Christ's **spiritual** Sonship become **literal**. Then the Father could declare, *"Thou art my Son, this day have I begotten thee"*. Paul takes it a step further in the same verse by saying, *"And again, I will be to him a Father, and he shall be to me a*

Son..." [1] Can you see how the Father and Son relation is symbolic? He says I will be **to you** a Father and you will be **to me** a Son!

But just to be certain, let's get a third witness. In the book of Acts we find that Paul uses this verse again, and applies it in the same way:

> *"God hath fulfilled the same unto us their children, in that he hath raised up Jesus again; as it is also written in the second psalm, Thou art my Son, this day have I begotten thee."* [2]

Once again we find the same verse being quoted and applied in the same way. When Christ returned to heaven, the Father said to Christ, *"Thou art my Son, this day have I begotten thee."*

Reading on in Hebrews chapter 1:

> *1:6 And again, when he bringeth in the first begotten into the world, he saith, And let all the angels of God worship him.*

So the Father brought in "the first begotten into the world"...where did He bring Him? The words "bringeth in" are translated from a Greek word "eisago" [3] which means "to introduce". ." So the structure of the verse goes like this:

When God the Father [*he*] introduced [*bringeth in*] Christ, who is [*the first begotten into the world*] he said, let all the angels of God worship him. This is taking about when Christ came back to heaven after He rose from the dead. The Father introduced Him to the angels as the now incarnate Christ and said *"Let all the angels of God*

---

1   Hebrews 1:5
2   Acts 13:33
3   Strong's number 1521

worship Him" as a sign that Jesus' offering had been accepted. It fits perfectly with the context of the rest of the chapter. Ellen White supports this interpretation:

*"As He enters Heaven, the angels hasten to do Him homage, but He waves them back, and going to His Father makes the plea, "Father, I will that they also whom thou hast given Me, be with Me where I am; that they may behold My glory, which Thou hast given Me; for Thou lovedst Me before the foundation of the world." What is the Father's answer?—"**And let all the angels of God worship Him.**" The pledge made before the foundation of the world is renewed. Christ's relation to His Father embraces all who receive Him by faith as their personal Saviour."* [1]

*"The voice of God is heard proclaiming that justice is satisfied. Satan is vanquished. Christ's toiling, struggling ones on earth are "accepted in the Beloved." Ephesians 1:6. Before the heavenly angels and the representatives of unfallen worlds, they are declared justified. Where He is, there His church shall be. "Mercy and truth are met together; righteousness and peace have kissed each other." Psalm 85:10. The Father's arms encircle His Son, and the word is given, "**Let all the angels of God worship Him.**" Hebrews 1:6."* [2]

We can see that the context of this chapter is after the incarnation. It has nothing to do with Christ being born of God in the past.

Paul refers to this same concept in Romans chapter one.

"Paul, a servant of Jesus Christ, called to be an apostle, separated unto the gospel of God,

2 (Which he had promised afore by his prophets in the holy scriptures,)

3 Concerning his Son Jesus Christ our Lord, which was

1   Bible Echo, May 22, 1899 par. 6
2   Desire of Age p. 834

made of the seed of David according to the flesh;
4 And declared to be the Son of God with power, according
to the spirit of holiness, by the resurrection from the dead." [1]

For all these verses, it's clear that the incarnation, and particularly the resurrection, changed the relationship between the Father and Christ in some way.

From all this, I learned not to be so quick to jump to a conclusion when I read a verse, but to carefully consider its true meaning. Slowly but surely the light of truth was becoming clearer.

Understanding Eternity

Some of my former fellow Anti-trinitarians have looked at the Hebrew word for "eternal" and formulated a way of explaining the Bible and Spirit of Prophecy's use of the word. The Strong's Definition goes like this:

Eternal - H5769 From H5956; properly concealed, that is, the vanishing point; generally time out of mind (past or future), that is, (practically) eternity; frequentative adverbially (especially with prepositional prefix) always: - always (-s), ancient (time), any more, con-tinuance, eternal, (for, [n-]) ever (-lasting, -more, of old), lasting, long (time), (of) old (time), perpetual, at any time, (beginning of the) world (+ without end). Compare H5331, H5703. [2]

They conclude that because the word eternal means "out of mind" and "concealed", everything "in" eternity must be a mystery which cannot be understood. So they drop a curtain between where time ends and eternity begins. Everything behind that curtain we cannot see. So Christ could have been begotten by the Father in eternity past, and have emerged from behind this curtain, and still be eternal – because we cannot see into eternity. You may come across a diagram something like this to illustrate this concept:

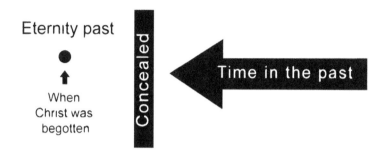

Though it may sound nice, sadly this concept is completely of human origin. I cannot find a single Bible text that sustains it. The only proof is Strong's Hebrew definition. However, let us not stop with the first half of the definition, let us read the whole thing. Read Strong's definition again, this time taking careful note of the words used after the underlined words. You will see descriptive words such as, "always", "continuance", "eternal", "perpetual", "without end". So eternity means a perpetual existence. You cannot be eternal and have a beginning.

What Is Eternity?

We are living in what we call "time". Time is governed by the earth's rotation, and by its movement around the sun.[1] It takes 24 hours for the earth to make a full 360° degree rotation on its axis, which equals a day. It takes the earth approximately 365 days to orbit the sun: this gives us a year.

Eternity, on the other hand, is not governed by these factors; it is not limited by days or years. When we read that someone is eternal, it doesn't mean they live "in" eternity, but that they "are" eternal.

....
1   Genesis 1:14

Consider this verse:

"Before the mountains were brought forth, or ever thou hadst formed the earth and the world, even from everlasting to everlasting, thou art God." [1]

Earlier we read that this Bible text applies to Christ. Think about the concept of eternity in the previous page and how it affects the meaning of this verse. It makes it meaningless. Instead of making Jesus eternal, it casts doubt on how long He has existed. Maybe He came into existence just behind the concealed line, and now He comes out and tells us He is eternal! What does that do to Jesus? We could also take it a step further and flip the illustration of time and eternity over into the future. It might look like this:

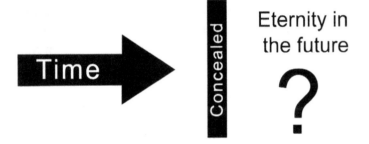

If this concept is true, how can we know that our eternal future is without end? If it is concealed from us, what stops us from saying that maybe sometime in the future of "eternity" our eternal life could end? What about God the Father? Maybe He also came into existence in the past eternity? How can we be sure of His eternal existence? Where is our rock solid testimony that God does not lie?

This destroys the beauty and simplicity of the Bible. Not only that, but it totally destroys the meaning of the word 'eternal'. If we believe that interpretation, then the word 'eternal' does not mean eternal anymore. It is a mystery that we cannot understand.

....
1   Psalm 90:2

What does the "vanishing point" mean then, I wondered? What was James Strong trying to say in his definition? All was made plain when I read this statement:

"In speaking of His pre-existence, Christ carries the mind back through dateless ages. He assures us that there never was a time when He was not in close fellowship with the eternal God." [1]

Have you ever stood outside at night and looked up at the stars? Did you know there are millions of stars out there which you cannot see? Astronomers pointed the Hubble Space Telescope at a dark spot in space, and lo and behold; they found more stars! Why can't we see them? Because there is a vanishing point! The point at which our eyes cannot penetrate. In the same way eternity disappears into the vanishing point. It passes the limits of numbers, figures, days and years. We have to put a generic name to it: "infinity". God has not purposely hidden it from our view, it is just our short-sightedness as humans that limits our vision.

---
1   Signs of the Times, August 29, 1900 par. 15

Chapter 3

Misunderstood Texts on the Nature of Christ

Now that things were starting to make sense, certain Bible verses and Ellen White quotes started coming to my mind that seemed to contradict what I had discovered. Some quotes from the Bible and Spirit of Prophecy on the surface can be confusing, especially when you have preconceived ideas, as I did. So often I had to take a detour to study out a seemingly contradictory statement. So come with me on a slight detour to discover the meaning of some of the more challenging statements on inspiration.

Proverbs 8:22-30

"The LORD possessed me in the beginning of his way, before his works of old. I was set up from everlasting, from the beginning, or ever the earth was. When there were no depths, I was brought forth; when there were no fountains abounding with water. Before the mountains were settled, before the hills was I brought forth: While as yet he had not made the earth, nor the fields, nor the highest part of the dust of the world. When he prepared the heavens, I was there: when he set a compass upon the face of the depth:

When he established the clouds above: when he strength-
ened the fountains of the deep: When he gave to the sea his
decree, that the waters should not pass his commandment:
when he appointed the foundations of the earth: Then I was
by him, as one brought up with him: and I was daily his de-
light, rejoicing always before him." [1]

The interpretation which I used to put on this verse is that Jesus was "brought forth" into existence far back in the ages of eternity by the Father.

But on closer examination, I found there are some problems with this interpretation. Firstly, the gender of "wisdom" in this verse is female. So if we are going to take this literal, we'd have to say that Christ is female. Secondly, Christ is here personified as the wisdom of God. So if this is talking about Christ's beginning, then there must have been a time when God had no wisdom! Clearly this verse has to be speaking in a poetic sense, of something deeper.

Let's look at it again and find out what it does say, and what it doesn't say.

"The LORD possessed me in the beginning of his way, be-
fore his works of old..." [2]

"Possessed"

The word "possessed" in Proverbs 8:22 gives us the idea of com-plete oneness. Listen to the words of Jesus' prayer to the Father and you will see the similarities. *"And all mine are thine, and thine are mine..."* [3] and a few verses down He says, *"That they all may be one; as thou, Father, art in me, and I in thee..."* [4] When Jesus says that the Father possessed Him, it is a poetic way of speaking

1   Proverbs 8:22-30
2   Proverbs 8:22
3   John 17:10
4   Verse 21

of their complete oneness. Ellen White confirms this. After quoting Proverbs 8:22-27, she said:

*"There are light and glory in the truth that **Christ was one with the Father** before the foundation of the world was laid. This is the light shining in a dark place, making it resplendent with divine, original glory. This truth, infinitely mysterious in itself, explains other mysterious and otherwise unexplainable truths, while it is enshrined in light, unapproachable and incomprehensible."* [1]

Clearly, this verse is talking about the oneness of the Father and Christ.

Someone once asked a question that really got me thinking: When was the "beginning" of the Father's "way"? The words "of His way" come from a Hebrew word "derek" which means *"a road (as trodden); figuratively a course of life"*. [2] Which basically is the beginning of the Father's life. When was that? We know that the Father has always existed and there was never a time when He did not exist. So if He possessed Christ, or was one with Christ in the beginning of His way, (poetically speaking), Christ too has no beginning. Notice what the Spirit of Prophecy says:

*"In speaking of His pre-existence, Christ carries the mind back through dateless ages. He assures us that there **never was a time** when He was not in close fellowship with the*

....
1   1 Selected Messages p. 248
2   Strong's Hebrew Dictionary, number H1870

THINK ABOUT IT!

We often misunderstand information when it is presented to us, because we have a preconceived mindset. Learning to read exactly want the quote says and doesn't say, is a skill that you can learn, with the Holy Spirit's help. That's why we need to always pray before we study!

*eternal God. He to whose voice the Jews were then listen-
ing had been with God **as one brought up with Him.**"* ¹

That last highlighted phrase comes from Proverbs 8:30. We are told
that there was **never a time** when Jesus was not "possessed" or one
with the Father. The next verse speaks even more clearly:

*"I was set up from **everlasting**, from the beginning, or ever
the earth was."* ²

"Setup"

The word "setup" means "pour out" or "anoint". So Jesus is saying
that He was anointed "from everlasting", or from eternity in the past.
This lines up with the quote we studied earlier:

*"God and Christ knew from the beginning, of the apostasy of
Satan and of the fall of Adam through the deceptive power
of the apostate. The plan of salvation was designed to re-
deem the fallen race, to give them another trial. **Christ was
appointed to the office of Mediator from the creation of
God, set up from everlasting to be our substitute and
surety.** Before the world was made, it was arranged that the
divinity of Christ should be enshrouded in humanity. "A body,"
said Christ, "hast thou prepared me" (Hebrews 10:5). But He
did not come in human form until the fullness of time had
expired. Then He came to our world, a babe in Bethlehem."* ³

Could it be that this verse is talking about the time when Christ was
appointed to the office of our Substitute and Saviour? Remember
how we discovered in the last chapter that Christ was anointed as
the Mediator of the Covenant from everlasting? Maybe this verse
has nothing to do with Christ's physical life? Remember that Solo-

....
1   Signs of the Times, August 29, 1900 par. 15
2   Proverbs 8:23
3   Selected Messages Vol.1, p. 250

mon is writing in a poetic style, speaking of wisdom, personified as Christ. He is not trying to say that Christ had a beginning. In fact, he is trying to emphasise the fact that Christ existed before all things and is eternal.

"Brought forth"

"When there were no depths, I was brought forth; when there were no fountains abounding with water." [1]

"Brought forth" are the only words in this passage that give some kind of indication to birth. The Hebrew word is "chuyl". The primary uses in the Bible for this word refer to "waiting" or being "in pain". Bring both these concepts together and you get a picture of a woman in labour, waiting for her baby to be born. But we know that painful births were a result of sin, so this has nothing to do with physical birth, in this context. But it does fit with the concept of Christ being appointed or setup as our Saviour in eternity past.

In fact, the point that these verses are trying to convey is the truth that Christ is pre-existent. If you read the context of all of the Ellen White statements that quote these verses, you will find that every one of them is talking about Christ's pre-existence. We know from all the evidence we've looked at so far, that Christ was not physically "born" before the creation of the world. But He did take on the role of our Saviour and Redeemer from eternity past, long before the depths or the earth itself was established.

This verse is not a good verse to use to base a belief system on, because the language is very poetic and we need more verses to support it before it can become a solid truth.

The Father the Head of Christ?

"But I would have you know, that the head of every man is

1   Proverbs 8:24

Christ; and the head of the woman is the man; and the head of Christ is God." [1]

The Father is the head of Christ. Doesn't that mean that the Father is superior to the Son? No, not at all. Read the rest of the verse. In the husband and wife relationship, is either one necessarily greater, more powerful, on a higher level, longer-lived than the other? No. Notice Paul uses the husband and wife relationship, not the father and son relationship, to illustrate the Divine relationship. But nonetheless, in any relationship, someone has to lead, and God the Father has that role as the leader. But that does not make Him superior to the Son.

The same concept is brought out in 1 Corinthians 15:24-28:

"Then cometh the end, when he shall have delivered up the kingdom to God, even the Father; when he shall have put down all rule and all authority and power. For he must reign, till he hath put all enemies under his feet. The last enemy that shall be destroyed is death. For he hath put all things under his feet. But when he saith all things are put under him, it is manifest that he is excepted, which did put all things under him. And when all things shall be subdued unto him, then shall the Son also himself be subject unto him that put all things under him, that God may be all in all." [2]

The Bible also says,

"I saw in the night visions, and, behold, one like the Son of man came with the clouds of heaven, and came to the Ancient of days, and they brought him near before him. And there was given him dominion, and glory, and a kingdom, that all people, nations, and languages, should serve

....
1   1 Corinthians 11:3
2   1 Corinthians 15:24-28

him: his dominion is an everlasting dominion, which shall not pass away, and his kingdom that which shall not be destroyed." [1]

Jesus tells us that the Father has *"given him authority to execute judgment also, because he is the Son of man."* [2] Christ's kingdom is an everlasting kingdom, so it doesn't get taken away from Him. But, as we read in 1 Corinthians 15:24-28, when the victory is won and the saints are in heaven, Jesus gives back judgment and leadership of the Kingdom to the Father, who is the leading figure in the Godhead. It doesn't mean that Jesus is of less authority or power than the Father.

You will find this thought of Jesus submitting to the Father running through the whole Bible. In the past, I used this to prove that Jesus is the literal son of God. But this is only a misunderstanding of the Godhead. There is perfect order in the Godhead, and to have perfect order, everyone must have roles or jobs to do. Just like in the family relation, everyone has a place, but all are of the same value and ability.

Christ can do Nothing of Himself?

"I can of mine own self do nothing: as I hear, I judge: and my judgment is just; because I seek not mine own will, but the will of the Father which hath sent me." [3]

This verse and others like it are often used to prove that Jesus is not self existent and derives His life from the Father. But the people quoting these verses do not consider the context.

All the statements of Jesus expressing His total reliance on His

....
1   Daniel 7:13,14
2   John 5:27
3   John 5:30

Father were said when He was incarnate on earth. As God, Christ is all powerful and self existent. But in order to be our example in everything, He chose to put aside His own power and rely totally on His Father.

God Cannot be Tempted?

"Let no man say when he is tempted, I am tempted of God: for God cannot be tempted with evil, neither tempteth he any man:" [1]

The question is sometimes asked in connection with this verse, "How can Jesus be the same God as the Father, if He cannot be tempted? For we know that Jesus was tempted in all points like us?"

May I ask another question? Can Jesus be tempted now, in heaven as God? No, of course not. Jesus was tempted in His humanity to use His Divine power, but it wasn't the Divine nature that was tempted. Indeed, when Jesus' Divine power did flash through His humanity, Satan had to leave.

Does the Father Only have Immortality?

*"That thou keep this commandment without spot, unrebukeable, until the appearing of our Lord Jesus Christ: Which in his times he shall shew, who is the blessed and **only Potentate**, the King of kings, and Lord of lords; Who **only hath immortality**, dwelling in the light which no man can approach unto; whom no man hath seen, nor can see: to whom be honour and power everlasting. Amen."* [2]

I always believed that this verse was talking about the Father as

....
1   James 1:13
2   1 Timothy 6:14–16

being the only Potentate who has immortality. But once I studied into it, I found I was completely wrong. If you read the verse before it reads:

*"I give thee charge in the sight of God, who quickeneth all things, and before **Christ** Jesus, who before Pontius Pilate witnessed a good confession...Which in his times he shall shew, who is the blessed and only Potentate"* [1]

It is actually speaking about both the Father and the Son, but the One who is going to be revealed at the end as the only Potentate on earth is Christ. Cross-referencing the wording with other verses, we find:

"These shall make war with the Lamb, and the Lamb shall overcome them: for he is Lord of lords, and King of kings: *and they that are with him are called, and chosen, and faithful."* [2]

"And he hath on his vesture and on his thigh a name written, KING OF KINGS, AND LORD OF LORDS.*"* [3]

Who is the King of kings, and Lord of lords? Jesus Christ. But just to be 100% certain that we are on the right track, let us look at Spirit of Prophecy:

*"Self is exalted, and Jesus, the blessed and **only Potentate**, the Mediator between God and man, does not work with them. Satan's insinuations are credited, and God's plain command in regard to mercy and tender compassion is ignored."* [4]

....

1   Verse 13,15
2   Revelation 17:14
3   Revelation 19:16
4   21 Manuscript Release p. 455

*"I am the resurrection, and the life." This language can be used only by the Deity. All created things live by the will and power of God. They are dependent recipients of the life of the Son of God. However able and talented, however large their capabilities, they are replenished with life from the Source of all life. **Only He who alone hath immortality,** dwelling in light and life, could say, "I have power to lay down my life, and I have power to take it again." All the human beings in our world take their life from Him. He is the spring, the fountain of life.* [1]

I was convinced: Jesus is the One being referred to in 1 Timothy 6:15,16. This is not to say that the Father is not immortal or the only potentate. The fullness of the Godhead dwells in the Father, Son and Holy Spirit.

Jesus "Came Out" of The Father?

"For the Father himself loveth you, because ye have loved me, and have believed that I came out from God. I came forth from the Father, and am come into the world: again, I leave the world, and go to the Father." [2]

Some of my well-meaning Anti-trinitarian friends have used the Greek meaning of the words "came forth" to prove that Jesus literally came out of the Father. But on closer examination, I found that the wording of the sentence doesn't fit with this theory. Jesus didn't come out of the Father and then go straight down to earth. The fact is, that Jesus left the heavenly courts, and came down to this earth as a baby. This has nothing to do with Him physically coming out of the Father.

The Greek word that they are using is "exerchomai":

....
1   MS 131, 1897, 5 Bible Commentary p. 1113
2   John 16:27,28

"From G1537 and G2064; to issue (literally or figurative-ly): - come-(forth, out), depart (out of), escape, get out, go (abroad, away, forth, out, thence), proceed (forth), spread abroad." [1]

If we look at how this word is used in the Bible, most of the time it is talking about leaving one place and going somewhere else. It does not mean physical birth. This is putting into the verse something that is not there.

The Spirit of Prophecy

Equally misunderstood are some portions of Spirit of Prophecy. As an Anti-trinitarian I was lead to believe that there are contradictions in Ellen White's writings. But I have since learned that this is not so. There is perfect harmony in Inspiration. It is only our own mis-understandings that get in the way.

Not Created, but Begotten?

"God so loved the world, that he gave his only-begotten Son,"-- not a son by creation, as were the angels, nor a son by adoption, as is the forgiven sinner, but a Son begotten in the express image of the Father's person, and in all the brightness of his majesty and glory, one equal with God in authority, dignity, and divine perfection. In him dwelt all the fullness of the Godhead bodily." [2]

This quote to me was one of the so-called "clincher" statements that proved my former belief. It is maintained that this quote shows clearly that Jesus was not created, but came into existence by the Father. It is therefore affirmed that this quote shows that "created" and "begotten" are not the same thing. But is this true? I had to find out.

....
1   Strong's Greek Dictionary, number 1831
2   Signs of the Times, May 30, 1895 par. 3

So I read the quote again and carefully considered each point with an open objective mind. To my surprise, I found a big hole in the interpretation. This is the rationale, according to Anti-trinitarians: Far back in the ages of eternity, the Father begat a Son. Not a Son by creation, like the angels: in other words, not created out of nothing. Not a Son by adoption: what does that mean? Is she suggesting that God might have adopted another being to be His Son? An angel perhaps? How absurd! Why would Ellen White even think of writing something like that? Or maybe we have actually missed what she is really saying. What is the point she is really trying to make? Let's read the context.

"There is but one way of escape for the sinner. There is but one agency whereby he may be cleansed from sin. He must accept the propitiation that has been made by the Lamb of God, who taketh away the sins of the world. The shed blood of Christ cleaseth us from all sin. "For he hath made him to be sin for us, who knew no sin; that we might be made the righteousness of God in him." "Him hath God exalted with his right hand to be a Prince and a Saviour, for to give repentance to Israel, and forgiveness of sins." A complete offering has been made; for "God so loved the world, that he gave his only-begotten Son,"-- not a son by creation, as were the angels, nor a son by adoption, as is the forgiven sinner, but a Son begotten in the express image of the Father's person, and in all the brightness of his majesty and glory, one equal with God in authority, dignity, and divine perfection. In him dwelt all the fullness of the Godhead bodily." [1]

The whole paragraph, and the whole article for that matter, is talking about Christ and His Incarnation. In the first half of the article Ellen White is writing about the Incarnation and the need of a complete offering to save humanity. Why should she then skyrocket into the past, and start talking about the time when Jesus was "begotten"?

....
1   Signs of the Times, May 30, 1895 par. 3

It is out of context; Ellen White is not trying to give us a lesson on where Christ came from, she is talking about Christ's sacrifice on earth.

So what was needed for the salvation of man was a real complete sacrifice. Not a created being, with the Divine Spirit of Christ put into it, not an adopted person with Divinity placed in it, but what was needed was Jesus, God Himself, to be begotten, born, literally, by Mary, through the power of the Holy Spirit. That human being born to Mary was the One who was in *"the brightness of his majesty and glory, one equal with God in authority, dignity, and divine perfection"*. Doesn't that make more sense? It is the only explanation that fits with the context. Let's compare this thought with another statement Ellen White made on the same topic and see if there is a connection.

"In contemplating the incarnation of Christ in humanity, we stand baffled before an unfathomable mystery, that the human mind cannot comprehend. The more we reflect upon it, the more amazing does it appear. How wide is the contrast between the divinity of Christ and the helpless infant in Bethlehem's manger! How can we span the distance between the mighty God and a helpless child? And yet the Creator of worlds, he in whom was the <u>fulness of the Godhead bodily</u>, was manifest in the helpless babe in the manger. Far higher than any of the angels, <u>equal with the Father in dignity and glory</u>, and yet wearing the garb of humanity! Divinity and humanity were mysteriously combined, and man and God became one. It is in this union that we find the hope of our fallen race. Looking upon Christ in humanity, we look upon God, and see in him the <u>brightness of his glory, the express image of his person</u>." [1]

So right here on earth, when Jesus was in human flesh, He was still God. In that baby laying in the manager was all the fullness of

------

1   ST, July 30, 1896 par. 3

the Godhead bodily. Wow! As He walked the earth, He was equal with the Father in dignity and glory, yet He said, not my will but thine be done. Can you see the connection between this quote and the one we read earlier? Go back and read it again, and look for the underlined phrases in the first quote. The "complete offering" that was made, was Jesus, the Divine-human Son of God. Jesus had to be the real genuine God on earth: not some make-believe created or adopted Son, but God Himself, born in the flesh. This perfectly harmonizes with everything we have discovered so far.

Was Jesus "Made" Equal with the Father?

"God is the Father of Christ; Christ is the Son of God. To Christ has been given an exalted position. He has been made equal with the Father. All the counsels of God are opened to His Son." [1]

Here was another "clincher" for me. But, we have just been reading that, *"From all eternity Christ was united with the Father, and when He took upon Himself human nature, He was still one with God."* [2]

Once again, the key to understanding Ellen White is to read the full context of the quote.

"Christ took with Him to the heavenly courts His glorified humanity. To those who receive Him, He gives power to become the sons of God, that at last God may receive them as His, to dwell with Him throughout eternity. If, during this life, they are loyal to God, they will at last "see His face; and His name shall be in their foreheads." Revelation 22:4. And what is the happiness of heaven but to see God? What greater joy could come to the sinner saved by the grace of Christ than to look upon the face of God and know Him as Father?

1   Testimonies for the Church Vol. 8 p. 268
2   1 Selected Messages p. 228

> *"The Scriptures clearly indicate the relation between God and Christ, and they bring to view as clearly the personality and individuality of each.*
> (Hebrews 1:1-5 quoted)
> *God is the Father of Christ; Christ is the Son of God. To Christ has been given an exalted position. He has been made equal with the Father. All the counsels of God are opened to His Son."* [1]

Can you see how that the context explains the quote? Ellen White is talking about Christ receiving back His position with the Father, after His unity was broken up at His death on the cross. Now their relationship takes on a new dimension. Now Christ is literally the Son of God, and the Father is literally the Father of Christ, because Jesus is God, incarnate in the flesh. He still holds that glorified human body today.

Ellen White is speaking in the context of Hebrews chapter 1. We covered Hebrews 1 in the last chapter and saw that its context is the incarnation. This clearly fits with Ellen White's usage of this verse.

Was Jesus Exalted above Lucifer?

> *"He (Lucifer) was beloved and reverenced by the heavenly host, angels delighted to execute his commands, and he was clothed with wisdom and glory above them all. Yet the Son of God **was exalted above him**, as one in power and authority with the Father. He shared the Father's counsels, while Lucifer did not thus enter into the purposes of God. "Why," questioned this mighty angel, "should Christ have the supremacy? Why is He honored above Lucifer?"* [2]

This passage is clearly explained a few pages later:

....
1   Testimonies for the Church Vol. 8 p. 268
2   Patriarchs and Prophets p. 36

"There had been no change in the position or authority of Christ. Lucifer's envy and misrepresentation, and his claims to equality with Christ, had made necessary a statement of the true position of the Son of God; but this had been the same from the beginning." [1]

Christ always had His position and authority, but because of Lucifer's doubt, it was necessary to re-establish Christ's position in the minds of all the angels.

"The First-born of Heaven"

"The dedication of the first-born had its origin in the earliest times. God had promised to give the First-born of heaven to save the sinner. This gift was to be acknowledged in every household by the consecration of the first-born son. He was to be devoted to the priesthood, as a representative of Christ among men." [2]

So, there we have it, Jesus is the First-born of heaven, so this means He was born literally of the Father in eternity? Does it really say that? Not at all. I'd like you to notice that Christ is the First-born of heaven, not of God the Father. Heaven includes the angels. Christ was heaven's gift: heaven's best. In the Hebrew culture the first born was the most important, the best: so they were asked to give their best to God, just as God would give His best for us.

There is only one place in the Bible when Jesus is said to be born, and that is in Bethlehem: nowhere else. So, doesn't it make sense to say that Jesus became the first born of heaven when He was born on earth? We cannot read into a verse what is not there.

....
1   Patriarchs and Prophets p. 37, 38
2   Desire of Ages p. 51

What is the Conclusion of the Matter?

From all this, I concluded that the idea that Christ was literally begotten/made/generated/created by the Father was false. It is a man-made theory that tries to explain the things of God in a way that appeals to our natural emotions. But God does not want us to rely on our feelings. He wants us to accept what He has told us in the Bible by faith and believe it. This enables us to rise above the level of humanity.

The Bible and Spirit of Prophecy clearly say that Jesus is divine, eternal, and self-existent. We are told that His life was not derived from any other being. He has always existed. Inspiration does not tell us that Jesus had a beginning. In fact it strongly asserts the opposite. Therefore, we only have one option: to accept what the Word of God says, regardless of our inability as humans to understand fully the mystery of God.

Jesus is the only begotten Son of God, there is absolutely no question or doubt about that. But to take the next step and say that Jesus is the literal birthed Son of God is like saying that Jesus is literally a lamb standing before the throne of God. What the Bible tells us is all we can and should believe. Anything more than this is taking things into our own hands.

I have not covered every possible argument in the debate on the nature of Christ, nor do I intend to. What I have done is given you the principles that God showed me so you can study this out for yourself.

After looking at all these quotes objectively, I am convinced: Jesus is God in every sense of the word. Let us exalt Christ to His rightful position as eternal God, unchanging, without end or beginning, self-existent, and all-powerful. He is now one with the human race, and promises to empower us with His own eternal, unlimited power!

Chapter 4

The Holy Spirit

Equally as confusing and misleading as the teachings regarding the nature of Christ, are the various teachings regarding who or what is the Holy Spirit? Ask this question to any Bible believing Christian and you are likely to get one of the following answers:

1. He is a physical being like the Father and the Son.
2. He is like the Father and Son, but different in that he doesn't have a physical body.
3. He is not a person at all, but the very essence of what God is (His power, personality, glory, presence) with no solid substance.
4. He is a force which fills all creation.
5. The Holy Spirit is a mystery that we cannot understand.
6. And you might even have someone tell you that the Holy Spirit is the angel Gabriel.

I stood back and asked, amongst all this confusion, where does the truth lie? After much study, I came to the conclusion that we are asking the wrong questions, and therefore getting the wrong answers. Instead of asking who or what is the Holy Spirit, we should be asking, what does inspiration tell us about the Holy Spirit. Ellen White is actually very clear in this area.

> *"It is **not essential** for us to be able to **define just what the Holy Spirit is**..."* [1]

....
1   Acts of the Apostles p.52

I had read this statement many, many times. But this time, I stopped and carefully thought about each word. My thoughts ran like this: If it is not essential to define just what the Holy Spirit is, then have we been trying to do something which we are not meant to do? Something that is impossible? I kept reading:

> *"...Christ tells us that the Spirit is the Comforter, "the Spirit of truth, which proceedeth from the Father." It is plainly declared regarding the Holy Spirit that, in His work of guiding men into all truth, "He shall not speak of Himself." John 15:26; 16:13.*
> *The **nature** of the Holy Spirit is a mystery. Men **cannot** explain it, because the Lord has not revealed it to them..."* [1]

I stopped and thought again: The nature of the Holy Spirit is not revealed to us. We cannot explain it. Is it then any wonder that there is so much confusion around this topic? We need to be careful. I think many of us need to take off our shoes, and remember that we are venturing on holy ground. This is not an area that God meant us to delve into. I read some more:

> *"...Men having fanciful views may bring together passages of Scripture and put a human construction on them, but the acceptance of these views will not strengthen the church. Regarding such mysteries, which are too deep for human understanding, silence is golden... the acceptance of these views will not strengthen the church."* [1]

This is so true. I have personally seen it many times. People who accept such views often end up leaving the church.

Writing to a man who had studied the Holy Spirit and come up with his own ideas, Ellen White wrote,

....
1   Acts of the Apostles p.52

"Your ideas of the two subjects you mention do not harmonize with the light which God has given me. The nature of the Holy Spirit is a mystery not clearly revealed, and you will never be able to explain it to others because the Lord has not revealed it to you. You may gather together scriptures and put your construction upon them, but the application is not correct. The expositions by which you sustain your position are not sound. You may lead some to accept your explanations, but you do them no good, nor are they, through accepting your views, enabled to do others good...

*....**There are many mysteries which I do not seek to understand or to explain; they are too high for me, and too high for you.** On some of these points, silence is golden. Piety, devotion, sanctification of soul, body, and spirit--this is essential for us all."* [1]

I asked myself: if there were things that God's messenger would not seek to understand, should we then try to seek them out?

Does this mean then that we should put a taboo sign on the Holy Spirit and don't talk about this issue at all? Absolutely not! But, we are given a strong caution, and some boundary lines. This is what we are clearly told.

Exactly "what" the Holy Spirit is, or the Nature of the Holy Spirit is not revealed to man. We cannot understand it.

However, Ellen White tells us that there are areas of the Holy Spirit which are "distinctly specified".

"The office of the Holy Spirit is distinctly specified in

....
1   Manuscript Release Vol 14, p 179

the words of Christ: "When He is come, He will reprove the world of sin, and of righteousness, and of judgment." John 16:8. It is the Holy Spirit that convicts of sin. If the sinner responds to the quickening influence of the Spirit, he will be brought to repentance and aroused to the importance of obeying the divine requirements." [1]

Earlier she said *"It is **plainly declared** regarding the Holy Spirit that, in **His work** of guiding men into all truth..." [1]*

Here we have two things that we can safely study regarding the Holy Spirit: His "office" and His "work". So I made up my mind to follow the guidelines written in Inspiration and study what is distinctly specified in the Word, and leave the speculation out.

So I did just that. I went to my computer, and did a word search for "Spirit" and "Ghost". - all 558 references! From all this I found that God has given us enough information about the Holy Spirit for us to understand his work and a few things which tell us what He is not. It gives us some clues as to what form the Holy Spirit has. But as to the details of who and exactly what the Holy Spirit is, it is silent. This is what I found:

What does the Bible say about the Holy Spirit?

The Holy Spirit had a part to play in Creation:
*"In the beginning God created the heaven and the earth. And the earth was without form, and void; and darkness was upon the face of the deep. And the **Spirit of God moved** upon the face of the waters." [2]*

Can carry a person away:
*"And he put forth the form of an hand, and took me by a lock of mine head; and the **spirit lifted me up** between the*

1   Acts of the Apostles p.52
2   Genesis 1:1,2

earth and the heaven, and brought me in the visions of God to Jerusalem..." [1]

Was involved in the Incarnation:
*"Now the birth of Jesus Christ was on this wise: When as his mother Mary was espoused to Joseph, before they came together, she was found **with child of the Holy Ghost.**"* [2]

Was present at Jesus' baptism:
*"And Jesus, when he was baptized, went up straightway out of the water: and, lo, the heavens were opened unto him, and he saw the **Spirit of God descending like a dove**, and lighting upon him."* [3]

Lead Jesus from place to place when He was on earth:
*"Then was Jesus **led up of the Spirit** into the wilderness to be tempted of the devil."* [4]

Rejection of the Holy Spirit means eternal death:
*"Wherefore I say unto you, All manner of sin and blasphemy shall be forgiven unto men: but the **blasphemy against the Holy Ghost shall not be forgiven unto men.**"* [5]

The name of the Holy Spirit is what we are baptised under:
*"Go ye therefore, and teach all nations, baptizing them in the name of the Father, and of the Son, and **of the Holy Ghost**"* [6]

The Holy Spirit speaks through us when we are in need of help:
"But when they shall lead you, and deliver you up, take no thought beforehand what ye shall speak, neither do ye premeditate: but whatsoever shall be given you in that hour, that

1   Ezekiel 8:3
2   Matthew 1:18
3   Matthew 3:16
4   Matthew 4:1
5   Matthew 12:31
6   Matthew 28:19

*speak ye: **for it is not ye that speak, but the Holy Ghost.***" [1]

The Holy Spirit is a Comforter to us here on earth, now that Jesus has left earth to go to His Father:

*"If ye love me, keep my commandments. And I will pray the Father, and he shall give you another Comforter, that he may abide with you forever; **Even the Spirit of truth**; whom the world cannot receive, because it seeth him not, neither knoweth him: but ye know him; for he dwelleth with you, and shall be in you."* [2]

The Holy Spirit testifies of Jesus:
*"But when the Comforter is come, whom I will send unto you from the Father, even the **Spirit of truth,** which proceedeth from the Father, **he shall testify of me.**"* [3]

The Holy Spirit does not speak of Himself:
*"Howbeit when he, the Spirit of truth, is come, he will guide you into all truth: for he **shall not speak of himself;** but whatsoever he shall hear, that shall he speak: and he will show you things to come."* [4]

The Holy Spirit spoke through the Apostles at the day of Pentecost:
*"And they were all filled with the Holy Ghost, and began to speak with other tongues, as the **Spirit gave them utterance.**"* [5]

....

1   Mark 13:11
2   John 14:15-17
3   John 15:26
4   John 16:13
5   Acts 2:4

The Holy Spirit can be lied to:
"But Peter said, Ananias, why hath Satan filled thine heart to lie to the Holy Ghost, and to keep back part of the price of the land?" [1]

The Holy Spirit was a Witness of Jesus' death and resurrection:
"And we are his witnesses of these things; and so is also the Holy Ghost, whom God hath given to them that obey him." [2]

The Holy Spirit directed the disciples:
"Then the Spirit said unto Philip, Go near, and join thyself to this chariot." [3]

The Holy Spirit helps us express ourselves when we pray:
"Likewise the Spirit also helpeth our infirmities: for we know not what we should pray for as we ought: but the Spirit itself maketh intercession for us with groanings which cannot be uttered." [4]

The Holy Spirit has a mind:
"And he that searcheth the hearts knoweth what is the mind of the Spirit, because he maketh intercession for the saints according to the will of God." [5]

The Holy Spirit understands the things of God:
"For what man knoweth the things of a man, save the spirit of man which is in him? even so the things of God knoweth no man, but the Spirit of God." [6]

The Holy Spirit is Lord (or God):

....

1   Acts 5:3
2   Acts 5:32
3   Acts 8:29
4   Romans 8:26
5   Romans 8:27
6   1 Corinthians 2:11

*"Now the **Lord is that Spirit**: and where the Spirit of the Lord is, there is liberty."* [1]

The Holy Spirit communes with us:
*"The grace of the Lord Jesus Christ, and the love of God, and the **communion of the Holy Ghost**, be with you all. Amen."* [2]

The Holy Spirit can be grieved:
*"And **grieve not the holy Spirit of God**, whereby ye are sealed unto the day of redemption."* [3]

The Holy Spirit invites us to receive the water of life
"And the Spirit and the bride say, Come. And let him that heareth say, Come. And let him that is athirst come. And whosoever will, let him take the water of life freely." [4]

At the end of my research, I sat back and asked, What does all this tell us about the Holy Spirit? Reading these verses at face value, it seems apparent that the Holy Spirit has an individual mind and work. But to try and invent ways of explaining the Holy Spirit by breaking up words and studying the Greek and Hebrew is not the way to go about it. What we need to do is to simply read and believe what God has written. Ellen White says the <u>work</u> of the Holy Spirit is "distinctly specified". If we study the Spirit's work, we will find out all we need to know. So with this in mind, I went deeper.

The Work Of The Holy Spirit.

My study revealed that the Bible has clearly laid out the work of the Holy Spirit in four main categories. They are:

1. Comforter

1   2 Corinthians 3:17
2   2 Corinthians 13:14
3   Ephesians 4:30
4   Revelation 21:6

2. Teacher
3. Reprover
4. Intercessor

Comforter

The Holy Spirit has been at work throughout the ages of earth's history, but after Christ's ascension, the Holy Spirit's work came to the forefront. He had a very important work to do. This work was to take over part of Jesus' role which He could not directly fulfil. Let's read about it:

Jesus said to His disciples, *"I go to prepare a place for you."* [1] He told them that He was going to *"pray the Father, and he shall give you another Comforter, that he may abide with you forever."* [2] And then, later on, He said: *"Nevertheless I tell you the truth; It is expedient for you that I go away: for if I go not away, the Comforter will not come unto you; but if I depart, I will send him unto you."* [3]

I asked, why was it so important that Jesus should go away and send the Comforter? Wasn't Jesus' presence enough? Why was "another" comforter needed? Ellen White gives us the answer.

> *"In taking our nature, the Saviour has bound Himself to humanity **by a tie that is never to be broken**. Through the eternal ages He is linked with us. "God so loved the world, that He gave His only-begotten Son." John 3:16. He gave Him not only to bear our sins, and to die as our sacrifice; He gave Him to the fallen race."* [4]

When Jesus took human nature and was born as a man, and ascended back to heaven, **He gave up His omnipresence.** No longer could

....

1   John 14:2
2   Verse 16
3   John 16:7
4   Desire of Ages p. 25

Jesus be in all places at all times. He is now tied to a human body. This was made clear when Jesus spoke to His disciples of what He was preparing for them.

> *"In my Father's house are many mansions: if it were not so, I would have told you. **I go** to prepare a place for you. And if **I go** and prepare a place for you, I will **come again,** and receive you unto myself; that **where I am**, there ye may be also."* [1]

Clearly, Jesus is up in heaven, and we are down on earth. Yet, Jesus clearly indicated that He would be with us always.[2] How can Christ be with us always, to comfort and encourage us, if He is tied to a human body that can only be in one place at a time? This problem had already been foreseen and solved by Divine Wisdom. Inspiration says:

....

1   John 14:2,3
2   *"Lo, I am with you alway, even unto the end of the world."* Matthew 28:20

APPLY IT TO YOUR LIFE!

"In taking our nature, the Saviour has bound Himself to humanity by a tie that is never to be broken. Through the eternal ages He is linked with us." (Desire of Age p. 25)

Stop and think about that. Jesus, the Almighty God, took on humanity. That blending of the Divine with the human was so close that it will stay like that for the rest of eternity! Now Jesus is tied to space and matter. He cannot be omnipresent—in all places at all times.

What an amazing sacrifice! Not only did He take a big risk and suffer so much pain and humiliation, but He gave up His omnipresence. Why? So that He can be closer to you and me. Doesn't that make your heart throb with loving a gratitude to Jesus?

*"The Holy Spirit is Christ's representative, but divested of the personality of humanity, and independent thereof. Cumbered with humanity, **Christ could not be in every place personally.** Therefore it was for their interest that He should go to the Father, and send the Spirit to be His successor on earth. No one could then have any advantage because of **his location** or **his personal contact** with Christ. By the Spirit the Saviour would be accessible to all. In this sense He would be nearer to them than if He had not ascended on high."* [1]

So the Holy Spirit is the answer. He would become the link that joins man with God. His work is to represent Christ. This is how He would be our comforter. Through the Holy Spirit, Christ would be divested of humanity. The tie is very close. We see this close connection in the book of Revelation: *"And I beheld, and, lo, in the midst of the throne and of the four beasts, and in the midst of the elders, stood a Lamb as it had been slain, having seven horns and **seven eyes, which are the seven Spirits of God sent forth into all the earth.**"* [2] Seven in the Bible represents completeness. We see here that the lamb (which is Christ) has seven eyes: these eyes represent the ministry of the Holy Spirit, allowing Him to "see" everywhere.

This brings me face to face with the question, is the Holy Spirit part of Christ, or is He an individual in His own right? The answer should be plain in that Christ said that He was **leaving**, and sending the Comforter. If Jesus was still here on earth, by His mind, then He wasn't really leaving, was He? Inspiration leaves no room for speculation on this question.

"Before this the Spirit had been in the world; from the very beginning of the work of redemption He had been moving

....
1   Desire of Ages p. 669
2   Revelation 5:6

upon men's hearts. But while Christ was on earth, the dis-ciples had **desired no other helper.** *Not until they were deprived of His presence would they feel their need of the Spirit, and then He would come."* [1]

When I discovered this quote, I was shocked. I couldn't believe I had not come across it before. Clearly Christ and the Holy Spirit are two separate Helpers.

"The Holy Spirit is the Comforter, in **Christ's name.** *He personifies Christ, yet is a* **distinct personality."** [2]

The Holy Spirit comes in the name of Christ. Therefore He cannot be Christ Himself, physically. It is clear that the Holy Spirit came in Christ's name as a **distinct personality.** The word distinct means:

DISTINCT, a. [L. See Distinguish.]
1. Literally, having the difference marked; separated by a visible sign, or by a note or mark; as a place distinct by name.
2. Different; separate; not the same in number or kind; as, he holds two distinct offices; he is known by distinct titles.
3. Separate in place; not conjunct; as, the two regiments marched together, but had distinct encampments.
4. So separated as not to be confounded with any other thing; clear; not confused. To reason correctly we must have distinct ideas. We have a distinct or indistinct view of a prospect. [3]

"The Holy Spirit **has** *a personality, else He could not bear witness to our spirits and with our spirits that we are the chil-dren of God. He must also be a divine person, else He could*

....
1   Desire of Ages p. 669
2   Manuscript Vol. 20, p. 324
3   Webster's 1828 Dictionary

not search out the secrets which lie hidden in the mind of God." [1]

Note: this quote says He **has** a personality. If the Holy Spirit has a personality, then He is a distinct individual.

"The Holy Spirit is a person, for He beareth witness with our spirits that we are the children of God." [2]

"...we need to realize that the Holy Spirit, who is as much a person as God is a person, is walking through these grounds, that the Lord God is our keeper, and helper." [3]

These words of Inspiration are so plain and simple, that there is no need to get confused. The Holy Spirit is not Christ. Yet, His presence is the same as Christ to us. Listen to what inspiration tells us:

"...the holy Spirit is the comforter, as the personal presence of Christ to the soul. [4]

The Holy Spirit would be to the disciples as, or *the same as*, the personal presence of Christ. They would not be able to feel the difference, because it is the same Godhead, the same Divine Power working through a different agent. This was a most beautiful gift.

"Christ determined that when He ascended from this earth He would bestow a gift on those who had believed on Him and those who should believe on Him. What gift could He bestow rich enough to signalize and grace His ascension to the mediatorial throne? It must be worthy of His greatness and His royalty. He determined to give His representative, the third person of the Godhead. This gift could not be ex-

1 Manuscript Vol 20, 1906, Evangelism p. 617
2 Ibid, Evangelism p. 616
3 Manuscript Release Vol 7, p. 299
4 Review and Herald, November 29, 1892 par. 3

celled. He would give all gifts in one, and therefore the divine Spirit, converting, enlightening, sanctifying, would be His donation." [1]

Christ has given Himself to mediating for us before the Father. Christ cannot do this, and be down on earth comforting us at the same time. Not because Christ is limited in power, but because of the limitation of a human body that He has accepted. This is the work of the Third Person of the Godhead. This is the gift that Christ gave to us. It is His donation.

"Of the Spirit Jesus said, "He shall glorify Me." The Saviour came to glorify the Father by the demonstration of His love; so the Spirit was to glorify Christ by revealing His grace to the world. The very image of God is to be reproduced in humanity. The honor of God, the honor of Christ, is involved in the perfection of the character of His people." [2]

This statement really impacted me. In the same way that Jesus came to reveal the Father to humanity, the Holy Spirit has come to reveal Christ to humanity. This proves without a shadow of a doubt that the Holy Spirit is not Christ. Unless we are to conclude that Jesus is part of the Father as well? The only way that Jesus could reveal the Father to us is in the fact that He was someone different to the Father. The only way that the Holy Spirit can reveal Jesus to us, if is He is different from Christ, just as Ellen White has so clearly stated.

If the Holy Spirit is part of Christ, His mind, character and omnipresence, then the sending of the Comforter is a fake.

I once read an article on the Holy Spirit in which the author main-

....
1   Signs of the Times, December 1, 1898 par. 2
2   Desire of Ages p. 671

tained that the Holy Spirit was the means by which the Father and the Son are omnipresent. Yet, Ellen White clearly says,

> *"Cumbered with humanity, Christ could not be in every place personally. Therefore it was for their interest that He should go to the Father, and send the Spirit to be His successor on earth."* [1]

If Christ was omnipresent through His Spirit before the incarnation, how is it that humanity prevented Him from being omnipresent after the incarnation? Did He give up His Spirit too? No. This is a great problem for this theory, because if the Holy Spirit is the mind and omnipresence of Christ, then the sending of the Comforter is all fake. Christ is still omnipresent like He has always been. There is no change caused by the Incarnation. But the Truth is plain. He truly did give up His omnipresence, and now the Holy Spirit is the link which enables Christ to connect humanity with divinity.

....
1   Desire of Ages p. 669

APPLY IT TO YOUR LIFE!

Isn't it amazing to read about how God has thought out and solved every possible problem that could ever exist? Jesus wanted to be close to us, and He did that by taking on humanity, forever. By doing this He created a big problem, because now He cannot be with us always. But God had the solution before the problem even existed! The Holy Spirit would become the link between heaven and earth.

God also has a solution for every problem that you have in your life—even before you have a problem, the answer is there! Ellen White says: *"Our heavenly Father has a thousand ways to provide for us, of which we know nothing."* (Desire of Ages p. 330)

Have you ever faced a problem where you could not see even one solution to the problem? Well, God has a thousand solutions!

Let's summarise what we have learned. The Holy Spirit:

- Is a separate helper from Christ.
- Comes in Christ's name.
- Does not speak of Himself
- Has a distinct personality.
- Is as much a person as God is a person.
- Is the same as the personal presence of Christ.
- Represents Christ, in the same way that Jesus represents the Father.

Looking at these characteristics, isn't it clear that, (a) the Holy Spirit is more then just the mind of the Father and the Son, and (b), the Holy Spirit is a person in His own right? You be the judge.

But there's more... that's just the first point. The Holy Spirit is also our...

Teacher

After assuring the disciples, though He was leaving them, He would send them the Comforter to take His place, Christ said:

> *"These things have I spoken unto you, being yet present with you. But the Comforter, which is the Holy Ghost, whom the Father will send in my name, he shall __teach you all things,__ and bring all things to your remembrance, whatsoever I have said unto you."* [1]

Then later on in John chapter 16 He said:

> *"I have yet many things to say unto you, but ye cannot bear them now. Howbeit when he, the Spirit of truth, is come, he will __guide you into all truth__: for he shall not speak of himself; but whatsoever he shall hear, that shall he speak:*

....
1   John 14:25,26

*and he will show you things to come. He shall glorify me: **for he shall receive of mine, and shall show it unto you.**" [1]*

Jesus made it very clear that the work of the Holy Spirit was to reveal to us truth. Specifically, He was to teach "all things", and "bring all things" that Jesus had taught them to their memory. He was to take what Christ said and give it to them in such a way that they would understand it. In other words, He would make the words of Christ come alive in their experience. Inspiration says:

*"How man can be a counterpart of Jesus Christ is beyond human comprehension. But the Holy Spirit can strengthen our spiritual eyesight, **enabling us to see what our natural eyes cannot see, or our ears hear, or our minds comprehend.** By the Spirit which searches all things, even the deep things of God, **have been revealed precious truths which cannot be described by pen or voice.** [2]*

The words of God can be written in pen and ink, or spoken by men of God, or even God Himself, yet they will not be fully understood, unless the Holy Spirit opens our understanding and reveals the light of truth to us in such as way that we will grasp it. As Paul says,

*"...it is written, Eye hath not seen, nor ear heard, neither have entered into the heart of man, the things which God hath prepared for them that love him. But God hath revealed them unto us **by his Spirit:** for the Spirit searcheth all things, yea, the deep things of God." [3]*

So in summary we can see that the Holy Spirit reveals to us the words of God so we can understand them. This is clear evidence that the Holy Spirit is a person with a distinct role. Listen to what

....

1   John 16:12-14
2   Sons and Daughters of God p. 34
3   1 Corinthians 2:9,10

inspiration says:

> *"The Holy Spirit has a personality, else He could not bear witness to our spirits and with our spirits that we are the children of God. He must also be a divine person, else He could not search out the secrets which lie hidden in the mind of God."* [1]

So, according to inspiration, in order for the Holy Spirit to fulfil this role as a teacher, He must be a "divine person". That's clear enough for me!

Reprover

Jesus told His disciples that when the Holy Spirit would come,

> *"...he will reprove the world of sin, and of righteousness, and of judgment: Of sin, because they believe not on me; Of righteousness, because I go to my Father, and ye see me no more; Of judgment, because the prince of this world is judged."* [2]

The word reprove in the margin means *"convince, or convict"*. Jesus listed three specific things that the Holy Spirit would convict the world of:

*   *"Of sin, because they believe not on me"* - Most of the world still did not believe in Jesus, but the Holy Spirit would continue the work that Jesus had started

*   *"Of righteousness, because I go to my Father, and ye see me no more"* - Once Jesus was gone, the work of calling men to righteousness needed to be continued. The Holy Spirit would do this work.

1   Manuscript 20, 1906, Evangelism p. 617
2   John 16:8-11

- *"Of judgment, because the prince of this world is judged."* - Jesus had won the victory, so now Satan's kingdom was doomed; and so were his followers, if they continued to follow Satan. So the Holy Spirit would convict hearts of the approaching judgment.

Once again it is clear to the open mind that in order for the Holy Spirit to perform this work, He must be a distinct person from Christ.

Intercessor

When I was first introduced to the idea of the Holy Spirit being an intercessor, I was indignant. I was quick to quote 1 Timothy 2:5, *"For there is one God, and **one mediator** between God and men, the man Christ Jesus."* [1] On further study I discovered that the Holy Spirit was indeed an intercessor, but He is not our Mediator. Christ is our only Mediator, but Paul tells us,

> *"Likewise the Spirit also helpeth our infirmities: for we know not what we should pray for as we ought: but the Spirit itself **maketh intercession** for us with groanings which cannot be uttered. And he that searcheth the hearts knoweth what is the mind of the Spirit, because he **maketh intercession** for the saints according to the will of God."* [2]

So the Holy Spirit does indeed intercede on for us. But notice what kind of intercession is mentioned here. We are told that the Holy Spirit helps us to pray, drawing out our true emotions and feelings, thus enabling us to fully express ourselves. Ellen White explains things better then I can:

> *"Christ, our Mediator, **and** the Holy Spirit are constantly interceding in man's behalf, but the Spirit pleads not for us as does Christ, who presents His blood, shed from the foundation of the world; the Spirit works upon our hearts, drawing*

....
1   1 Timothy 2:5
2   Romans 8:26,27

out prayers and penitence, praise and thanksgiving. The gratitude which flows from our lips is the result of the Spirit's striking the cords of the soul in holy memories, awakening the music of the heart." [1]

So we have two intercessors on our behalf. But both have very different roles. Christ on one hand is in heaven pleading His blood that was shed for us. On the other hand, the Holy Spirit is down on earth with us enabling us to receive and appreciate the blessings which Christ provides us, through His work in heaven.

This again is clear proof that the Holy Spirit is a separate person from Christ, with a distinct work.

"Christ in You, the Hope of Glory"

The apostle Paul stated that his calling was to declare *"the mystery which hath been hid from ages and from generations...which is **Christ in you**, the hope of glory."* [2] What does this really mean? How does Christ dwell in us? Some of my dear Anti-trinitarian brothers and sisters have declared that this verse is ultimate proof that the Holy Spirit is not a person, but the Spirit and essence of Christ. For, they reason, how can Christ dwell in us if He is a physical being? The answer, they claim, is that Christ imparts to us the Holy Spirit who is His mind and character. If the Holy Spirit were a person, how could He live inside us, they reason?

But is this true? Do they have a valid point, or is this a misunderstanding? Think about it: What is the sum total of Paul's teachings from Romans to Hebrews? Isn't it what Jesus is like and how we are to follow His example? Just study Philippians chapter 2 and it's plain what it means to have Christ dwelling in us. Let's look at a few verses from this chapter.

....
1   1 Selected Messages p. 344
2   Colossians 1:26, 27

"Let this mind be in you, which was also in Christ Jesus." [1]

Most Anti-trinitarians will tell you that to have the mind of Christ is to have the Holy Spirit dwelling in you. But this is not true. Sister White says:

"If the teachers have the mind of Christ and are being __molded__ by the Holy Spirit, they will be kind, attentive, and truly courteous." [2]

So in order to have the mind of Christ, we need to be **molded** by the Holy Spirit. The Holy Spirit is a person who does something in our lives. The Holy Spirit works to change our hearts and minds so that we are like Christ. He is not the mind of Christ, His work produces the mind of Christ in us. If we read the context of Philippians 2:5 we can clearly see this.

"Let nothing be done through strife or vainglory; but in lowli-

---

1   Philippians 2:5
2   Counsels to Parents, Teachers, and Students p. 270

APPLY IT TO YOUR LIFE!

In giving us the Holy Spirit, Jesus gave everything He could possibly give. He had already given everything He had at Calvary. Now that Jesus had risen from the dead and ascended to heaven, He gave Himself completely to the work of ministering in the sanctuary for us. And He is still ministering for us today. But that wasn't enough either. He didn't want to leave us down here without help and encouragement. So He sent the Holy Spirit to guide and direct us. We are told that the Holy Spirit is to us as the personal presence of Christ. Christ cannot be with us personally, because of what He has given up, but He has given us His presence through the ministry of the Holy Spirit.

Isn't that incredible? Jesus has given so much for you and me. What are you giving in return?

ness of mind let each esteem other better than themselves. Look not every man on his own things, but every man also on the things of others. Let this mind be in you, which was also in Christ Jesus: Who, being in the form of God, thought it not robbery to be equal with God: But made himself of no reputation, and took upon him the form of a servant, and was made in the likeness of men: And being found in fashion as a man, he humbled himself, and became obedient unto death, even the death of the cross." [1]

To have the mind of Christ is to think like Christ, to talk like Christ and to act like Christ. It is to be self-sacrificing, humble, and long-suffering, just as Christ is. But how do we know what Christ is like? By studying His life on earth. There He revealed perfectly what God is like, and He says, *"I have given you an example, that ye should do as I have done"* [2] Paul tells us that as we look at the *"glory of the Lord"* we *"are changed into the same image from glory to glory, even as **by** the Spirit of the Lord."* [3] So as we study the life of Christ and focus on Him, the Holy Spirit molds our mind so that we are changed into the same image or likeness of Christ. Thus, Christ is revealed in our words and acts. Those who look on us see not us, but Christ. They will conclude we have *"been with Jesus"* [4] and His life is our life. This is how Christ dwells in us. It is nothing complicated or mysterious. Anyone can understand it. Inspiration tells us,

*"As in humility they (the apostles) submitted to the **molding influence** of the Holy Spirit, they received of the **fullness of the Godhead** and were **fashioned in the likeness of the divine.**"* [5]

So we allow the Holy Spirit to mold our characters, we become like Christ. The Holy Spirit is not the life and power of God in us, but it

1   Philippians 2:3-8
2   John 13:15
3   2 Corinthians 3:18
4   Acts 4:13
5   Acts of the Apostles p. 49

is His work to impart that life and power to us.

If the Holy Spirit is the mind and power of God, we have a problem: Inspiration is very clear that the Holy Spirit is God. If we have the Holy Spirit in us (the mind and power of God, according to Anti-trinitarians) then we have God in us. This is very close to what Dr Kellogg taught in Ellen White's day (more on that in a later chapter) and also very close to what Satan said to Eve in the garden: *"Ye shall not surely die... ye shall be as gods, knowing good and evil."* [1] It is the beginnings of a spiritualistic mindset. Its a mindset that tries to put God in a box inside of us, when we need to realize how great God really is. God is a person, not a force, an influence, or a power. God has all of these things, but they aren't God.

In Summary

We have just taken a broad panoramic view of the work of the Holy Spirit as revealed in inspiration. We looked at four aspects of the Holy Spirit's work. We discovered how He reveals Christ to us, and His work as;

- Comforter
- Teacher
- Reprover
- Intercessor

From the truth we have just studied about the work of the Holy Spirit, it is clear that He has to be a separate and distinct person from the Father and the Son. But there were still some doubts in my mind from other texts that I have read that seemed to contradict what I had learnt so far. So I set out to find the true meaning of these so called "proof texts" that the Holy Spirit is not a person. What I found was astounding...

....
1   Genesis 3:4,5

Chapter 5

Misunderstood Texts on The Holy Spirit

There are many quotes in the Spirit of Prophecy and the Bible which, if taken out of their context, can be interpreted in the wrong way. Here are some quotes which have caused confusion and misunderstanding to me. What I am about to share with you is what the Lord showed me in my study. I recommend you study each one carefully yourself.

The Presence and Power of God?

"The divine Spirit that the world's Redeemer promised to send, is the presence and power of God." [1]

The presence and power of God? That does seem to support the Anti-triniarian Movement, I thought. But is that all? If we leave it here and don't read any further, we might come to this conclusion. But then I remembered another quote that sheds some light on this statement:

*"**Cumbered with humanity, Christ could not be in every place personally;** therefore it was altogether for their advantage that He should leave them, go to His father, and*

....
1   Signs of the Times, November 23, 1891 par. 1

*send the Holy Spirit to be **His successor** on earth. The Holy Spirit is Himself divested of the personality of humanity and independent thereof. He would represent Himself as present in all places by His Holy Spirit, as the Omnipresent. "But the Comforter, which is the Holy Ghost, whom the Father will send in My name, He shall (although unseen by you), [THIS PHRASE WAS ADDED BY ELLEN WHITE.] teach you all things, and bring all things to your remembrance, whatsoever I have said unto you" [John 14:26]. "Nevertheless I tell you the truth; It is expedient for you that I go away: for if I go not away, the Comforter will not come unto you; but if I depart, I will send Him unto you" [John 16:7].* [1]

Christ had to leave the disciples. He could not stay. Now He represents Himself by the Holy Spirit on earth. But the Holy Spirit is not Christ. Otherwise Christ would not be leaving. How can Christ be His own successor? Christ is cumbered with humanity. He cannot be in every place at once. So the Holy Spirit, is the presence and power of God with us now, every moment of the day. In this sense, the Holy Spirit is Christ, divested of humanity. The Holy Spirit is not Christ literally. But His presence and power is the same as the presence and power of Christ. Here is another quote that I used to use:

"In giving us His Spirit, God gives us Himself, making Himself a fountain of divine influences, to give health and life to the world." [2]

Isn't that a beautiful promise? When Christ sent the Holy Spirit, He was just as effectively giving Himself. It's got nothing to do with Christ sending His mind down here to be with us. The Holy Spirit, just as Spirit of Prophecy has clearly made known to us, is representing Christ. Yet, the unity of the Godhead is so close that it is the same as Christ being there personally.

....

1   14 Manuscript Release p. 23, non-italic words are mine
2   Testimonies for the Church Vol. 7 p. 273

"Christ declared that after his ascension, he would send to his church, as his crowning gift, the Comforter, who was to take his place. This Comforter is the Holy Spirit,--the soul of his life, the efficacy of his church, the light and life of the world. With his Spirit Christ sends a reconciling influence and a power that takes away sin." [1]

This is another beautiful, yet misunderstood quote. The Holy Spirit is to us, the soul of Jesus' life. What does this mean? It cannot mean that the Holy Spirit is Christ, because the sentence before that says that the Holy Spirit was to take Christ's place! How can Christ take His own place? "Soul" is old English for the "essence" or "chief part". So what this is saying is, the life of Christ is imparted to us through the Holy Spirit. The Holy Spirit gives to us the very essence of who Christ is.

"The influence of the Holy Spirit is the life of Christ in the soul. We do not now see Christ and speak to Him, but His Holy Spirit is just as near us in one place as another." [2]

The first two words of this quote clearly explain Ellen White's meaning. The **influence** of the Holy Spirit is the life of Christ in the soul. It does not say, The Holy Spirit is the Life of Christ in the soul--this is what Anti-trinitarians seems to see when they read this quote. But the word "influence" changes the whole meaning. This helps to clarify the quote we just read in Review and Herald. The Holy Spirit imparts the life of Christ to us. Christ cannot do this because He is not omnipresent: therefore, the only way the life of Christ can be imparted to us is by the Holy Spirit.

"...the holy Spirit is the Comforter, as the personal presence of Christ to the soul." [3]

....
1   Review and Herald, May 19, 1904 par. 1
2   Manuscript Release Vol. 2, p. 28
3   Review and Herald, November 29, 1892 par. 3

Notice that one little word "as"? That means "the same as". So the Holy Spirit is the same as the personal presence of Christ in the soul. This fits perfectly with the rest of Inspiration.

"Another Comforter"?

*"If ye love me, keep my commandments. And I will pray the Father, and he shall give you **another Comforter,** that he may abide with you forever; Even the Spirit of truth; whom the world cannot receive, because it seeth him not, neither knoweth him: but ye know him; for he dwelleth with you, and shall be in you."* [1]

In order to try and explain the meaning of the word "another" in this verse, some of my Anti-trinitarian friends have linked this verse with 1 Samuel 10:6,9:

*"And the spirit of the LORD will come upon thee (Saul), and thou shalt prophesy with them, and shalt be turned into **another man**...And it was so, that when he had turned his back to go from Samuel, God gave him **another heart:** and all those signs came to pass that day."* [2]

The reasoning is, Saul did not become a different person but there was a change in his heart.

The problem with the Anti-trinitarian reasoning is Jesus did not become "another" anything, when He ascended back into heaven. 1 Samuel 10:6 is speaking about a heart change, so that Saul became a different person. Jesus is the same forever. The only change was that His body was glorified. From the light we have looked at, it is quite clear that the "another" Comforter that Jesus promised to send is not Himself, but someone else, the Holy Spirit.

....
1   John 14:15-17
2   1 Samuel 10:6,9

What about "Parakletos"?

The word "comforter" in John 14:16 is the Greek word "paraklē-tos" which means, *"An intercessor, consoler: - advocate, comfort-er."* [1] The same word is used in 1 John 2:1

> *"My little children, these things write I unto you, that ye sin not. And if any man sin, we have an advocate (paraklētos) with the Father, Jesus Christ the righteous."* [2]

I once used this verse to prove that the Holy Spirit is the same as Christ. But Inspiration clearly tells us that both Christ and the Holy Spirit intercede on our behalf. Remember the quote we read before:

> *"Christ, our Mediator, **and** the Holy Spirit are constantly interceding in man's behalf, but the Spirit pleads not for us as does Christ, who presents His blood, shed from the foundation of the world; the Spirit works upon our hearts, drawing out prayers and penitence, praise and thanksgiving. The gratitude which flows from our lips is the result of the Spirit's striking the cords of the soul in holy memories, awakening the music of the heart."* [3]

This is irrefutable proof that the Holy Spirit is an individual person, separate from Christ. Both have totally different roles. Christ is in heaven, pleading His blood before the Father, and the Holy Spirit is pleading as well, but not as Christ does. He is down here with us, working on our hearts and drawing us to Christ. Therefore the Holy Spirit is an intercessor, and so is Christ: yet, their work is completely different.

....
1   Strong's Greek Dictionary, number G2889.
2   1 John 2:1
3   Selected Messages Vol. 1, p. 344

Spiritual Lethargy in the Church?

"The reason why the churches are weak and sickly and ready to die, is that the enemy has brought influences of a discouraging nature to bear upon trembling souls. He has sought to shut Jesus from their view as the Comforter, as one who reproves, who warns, who admonishes them, saying, 'This is the way, walk ye in it.'" [1]

This was another one of my former favourite proof texts. I used to take the position that, believing that the Holy Spirit is an individual is the cause of the spiritual lethargy in the church! But sadly, too often the same spiritual lethargy exists in the Anti-trinitarian circles. This is a terrible misapplication of the quote. The Holy Spirit being a person does not mean that Jesus is not our Comforter. Listen to what Ellen White wrote:

"Christ could not be in every place personally. Therefore it was for their interest that He should go to the Father, and send the Spirit to be His successor on earth. No one could then have any advantage because of his location or his personal contact with Christ. By the Spirit the Saviour would be accessible to all. In this sense He would be nearer to them than if He had not ascended on high." [2]

Jesus laid aside His Omnipresence. So the only way Jesus can be our Comforter is through the work of the Holy Spirit. The Holy Spirit is just as much our Comforter as Jesus is. For Satan to shut Jesus from our view as the Comforter, he must shut away the Holy Spirit from our minds with the busyness and cares of this life, or anything else that prevents us from hearing that Still Small Voice. We could become so busy teaching ideas and theories from the Bible, (even the Anti-trinitarian belief that the Holy Spirit is Christ) that we lose sight of Jesus as our Comforter (through the ministry of the Holy

....

1   Review and Herald, August 26, 1890 par. 10
2   Desire of Ages p. 669

Spirit). This has nothing to do with the nature of the Holy Spirit. Regardless of your theological understanding of who or what the Holy Spirit is, this quote may still apply to you. This is something to consider carefully.

"The Only Being in the Universe"

"Christ, the Word, the only begotten of God, was one with the eternal Father—one in nature, in character, in purpose--the only being that could enter into all the counsels and purposes of God." [1]

This quote is perhaps one of the most "conclusive" quotes that I used to prove that the Holy Spirit is not an individual person. The

1   Patriarchs and Prophets p. 3

APPLY IT TO YOUR LIFE!

What is the real reason for spiritual "Laodiceanism" in the church? Isn't it anything that draws our minds away from Christ? Satan is trying to shut Jesus from our eyes. He is making us argue about who the Holy Spirit really is, instead of focusing on the work of the Holy Spirit which is to reprove us of our sins and draw us to Christ. Notice what Inspiration says:

"All truth is found in Christ. 'Ye are complete in him.' Satan is continually seeking to turn minds away from Christ. Through his devices, man has been exalted, and has received confidence and honour that belong only to God. The people have looked to men for wisdom, instead of looking to God. And in order to save man from ruin, God has been compelled to let him see his own weakness by withdrawing, in a great measure, the Holy Spirit from him." (Review and Herald April 12, 1892, par. 2)

Here is the reason: because we have turned our minds from Christ, He has had to remove the Holy Spirit from us.

reasoning is, if Christ is the only being that can enter into the counsels of God, then the Holy Spirit must not be a being, or else He cannot enter into the counsels of God.

We can understand this quote, if we carefully study the context and compare it with other quotes. Reading elsewhere in the Spirit of Prophecy we find another, even clearer statement:

> *"The Godhead was stirred with pity for the race, and the Father, the Son, and the Holy Spirit gave Themselves to the working out of the plan of redemption. In order fully to carry out this plan, it was decided that Christ, the only-begotten Son of God, should give Himself an offering for sin."* [1]

It is very clear from this statement that the Holy Spirit, as a separate individual, did indeed have a part to play in the working out of the plan of salvation. So we need to read the context of the statement in question so we can discover what Ellen White is really saying.

Reading the context, we find that it is speaking about Lucifer and his aspirations to do the work that Christ was doing. The Father calls a meeting to set forth before the angels the rightful position of Jesus Christ:

> *"Before the assembled inhabitants of heaven the King declared that none but Christ, the Only Begotten of God, could fully enter into His* **purposes**, *and to Him it was committed to* **execute** *the mighty counsels of His will. The Son of God had* **wrought** *the Father's will in the creation of all the hosts of heaven; and to Him, as well as to God, their homage and allegiance were due. Christ was still to exercise divine power, in the creation of the earth and its inhabitants. But in all this He would not seek power or exaltation for Himself contrary to God's plan, but would exalt the Father's glory*

....
1   Review and Herald, May 2, 1912 par. 3

and **execute** *His purposes of beneficence and love."* [1]

Lucifer wanted to be involved in all the purposes of God. But God the Father clearly showed the angels that only Christ could do this. To "enter into" the purposes of God, means to **execute and fulfil the purposes of God**. Notice the highlighted words in the previous quote. When we read about Christ entering into God's purposes, we usually think of them sitting in a meeting room and talking and laying plans. But this is only part of the purposes of God. It also means to fulfill the plan by **putting it into action.**

Christ was the key person in the plan of Salvation. He was the one who came down to earth to represent the Father and to do His work. The Holy Spirit also had a part to play in the plan of salvation. His work, as we have already studied, came into effect fully after Jesus ascended to heaven. The Holy Spirit could not **fully** enter into or execute the Plan of Salvation in the same sense that Christ could. Only Christ was appointed to do this work. Christ was the one who became man, who lived the law of God, and died and rose from the dead. This is fully entering into and executing the plan of Salvation.

Ellen White uses this term *"to enter into the purposes of God"* in another place which makes the meaning clearer. *"The only safety for us is to **enter into the counsels of Heaven,** ever seeking to do the will of God, to become labourers together with him.* [2]

Can we go up into heaven and join in discussing the Plan of Salvation? No, of course not! But we can do the will of God and become labours together with Him. Then we become part of the great Plan of Redemption, and have entered into the counsels of heaven.

Getting back to our original quote, Christ was indeed the only being who could enter into and execute **all** the counsels and purposes of God. But this does not mean that the Holy Spirit could not en-

....
1   Patriarchs and Prophets p. 36
2   1888 Messages p. 903

ter into the counsels of Heaven as well. We ourselves can enter into God's plans. How much more can the Holy Spirit! Christ has a special work, so He has a special place in the Godhead. This does not make Him greater than the Holy Spirit or the Father: on the contrary, Christ completely submitted to the Father. But in humbling Himself, He has become highly exalted.

What is the Conclusion of the Matter?

Who or what is the Holy Spirit? Inspiration clearly tells us that the nature of the Holy Spirit is a mystery which we cannot understand. But, by looking at the work of the Holy Spirit, we know that the Holy Spirit is a separate individual from Christ and the Father. Is He a being just like the Father and Son, or does He take some other form? We don't know. It doesn't matter. What matters is, the Holy Spirit is a real, distinct individual separate from the Father and Christ who has a vital role to play in our salvation. On anything more than this, silence is golden.

Chapter 6

Understanding The Godhead

Thus far, the nature of Christ and the Holy Spirit were becoming very clear in my mind. Now I wanted to look at what inspiration had to say about the Godhead in general and see if my findings would match up here as well. If there are three distinct persons in the Godhead, we should be able to see this concept in the Bible's teachings about God.

So I concluded that the way to understand what God is like is to study God's character. The way to study God's character is to examine His law and the guidelines which He has given us. If God expects us to act in a certain way, we can be sure that He Himself will lead the way by example.

Self Sacrifice

The most foundational character trait of God's government is self sacrifice: esteeming others as better than yourself. We see this clearly in Philippians chapter two.

"Let nothing be done through strife or vainglory; but in lowliness of mind let each esteem other better than themselves.

Look not every man on his own things, but every man also on the things of others. Let this mind be in you, which was also in Christ Jesus: Who, being in the form of God, thought it not robbery to be equal with God: But made himself of no reputation, and took upon him the form of a servant, and was made in the likeness of men: And being found in fashion as a man, he humbled himself, and became obedient unto death, even the death of the cross." [1]

Jesus Christ clearly demonstrated this character trait when He came as a Man on this earth and died a cruel death.

The Father also demonstrated this attribute in giving His Son to die.

"For God so loved the world, that he gave his only begotten Son, that whosoever believeth in him should not perish, but have everlasting life." [2]

We see this same character trait revealed in the way Christ treated the Father.

"Then said Jesus unto them, When ye have lifted up the Son of man, then shall ye know that I am he, and that I do nothing of myself; but as my Father hath taught me, I speak these things. And he that sent me is with me: the Father hath not left me alone; for I do always those things that please him." [3]

Jesus always seeks to put the Father first, before Himself. This character trait is also revealed in how the Father treated Christ:

"But unto the Son he (the Father) saith, Thy throne, O God,

....
1 Philippians 2:3-8
2 John 3:16
3 John 8:28

*is forever and ever: a sceptre of righteousness is the scep-
tre of thy kingdom. Thou hast loved righteousness, and hated iniquity; therefore God, even thy God, hath anointed thee
with the oil of gladness above thy fellows. And, Thou, Lord,
in the beginning hast laid the foundation of the earth; and
the heavens are the works of thine hands: They shall perish; but thou remainest; and they all shall wax old as doth
a garment; And as a vesture shalt thou fold them up, and
they shall be changed: but thou art the same, and thy years
shall not fail."* [1]

Here we see the Father praising Christ for what He has done in the
Plan of Salvation and in the Creation of the world.

The Holy Spirit also reveals self-sacrifice:

*"Howbeit when he, the Spirit of truth, is come, he will guide
you into all truth: for he shall not speak of himself; but whatsoever he shall hear, [that] shall he speak: and he will show
you things to come. He shall glorify me: for he shall receive
of mine, and shall show it unto you."* [2]

The Holy Spirit does not even speak of Himself. His total focus is
revealing Christ.

This clearly shows the complete unity of the Godhead. They have
one purpose and each forgets about Themselves in fulfilling that
purpose. We should be the same in our lives. As families and as a
church, we all should forget self and focus on the mission God has
given us!

....

1   Hebrews 1:8-12
2   John 16:13,14

God is Love

Closely connected with self sacrifice is love. The Bible tells us that *"God is love"* [1]. Note that the verse does not say that God is **loving**, but that He **is** love. God is the complete expression of love. He is the definition of what love is. When we look at God, we can see love personified, love revealed in the ultimate example of what love is. God is the originator of love. If we want to know what love is, we need to study God. The love of God is revealed in the sacrifice made for you and me.

"God is love, in himself, in his very essence." [2]

"'God is love' (1 John 4:16). His nature, His law, is love. It ever has been; it ever will be. 'The high and lofty One that inhabiteth eternity' (Isaiah 57:15), whose 'ways are everlasting' (Habakkuk 3:6), changeth not. With Him 'is no variableness, neither shadow of turning' (James 1:17)." [3]

This gives us a clue as to what God is like. Even a casual reading of the Bible shows us that God is composed of more than one individual. The Spirit of Prophecy tells us that,

"The Sovereign of the universe was not alone in His work of beneficence. He had an associate--a co-worker who could appreciate His purposes, and could share His joy in giving happiness to created beings..." [4]

This highlights a principal that exists throughout creation:

....
1   1 John 4:8
2   Review and Herald, February 26, 1895 par. 2
3   Mind, Character, and Personality, vol 1, p. 247
4   Patriarchs and Prophets p. 34

Love Cannot be Self-centred

This means that in order to love unselfishly, you must have **someone to love**. This principal was apparent when God created man. He said, *"It is not good that the man should be alone; I will make him an help meet for him."* [1] You cannot love and be alone. *"Love cannot long exist without expression."* [2]

If Christ is eternal just like the Father, this makes perfect sense. But for the One True God movement, this poses a big problem. If there is only one eternal being in the Godhead, no matter how far back in eternity you go to when Jesus was 'begotten', there is still an infinity beyond when God was alone. This cannot be, for God is the complete expression of love, and true love cannot exist alone.

....
1   Genesis 2:18
2   Adventist Home p. 107

THINK ABOUT IT!

It has long been the charge of Anti-trinitarians that the belief in three divine, co-eternal beings destroys the beauty and depth of the love of God and the sacrifice He made. But as you can see from what we have been studying, this is far from the truth. The way the Godhead works in the plan of Salvation is mind blowing. It's so simple, yet profound and deeply significant.

To think that the eternal bond which exists in the Godhead, that is far greater than the closest father-son relationship, was torn apart at Calvary is just amazing. But what it takes is faith—faith to believe something I cannot fully understand. The Anti-trinitarian understanding does not require much faith: it appeals to our emotional side, and brings God down to our level. Must we do this in order to love and understand God? No! Let us take hold of the Word of God, and soar on the wings of faith to the heights that God wants us to attain to.

One God?

Yet, the Bible tells us, *"The LORD our God is one LORD."* [1] This text is often used to promote that there is only one person in the Godhead. Yet, we are given undeniable proof that there is more than one individual with the title of God. In the account of creation, we can see a pattern which gives a clue as to how the Godhead works. After God had created heaven, earth and all the creatures in it, the Bible says:

> *"And God said, Let **us** make man in our image, after **our** likeness..."* [2]

Yet, in the next verse we read:

> *"So God created man in **his** own image, in the image of God created **he** him; male and female created **he** them."* [3]

It is interesting how we have both the single and the plural mentioned here. This should be no enigma though, because the Bible clearly explains itself. Paul tells us that God *"created all things by Jesus Christ".* [4] So though we have more than one person speaking in Genesis 1:27, it is Christ who executes the decision.

So the Godhead says, *"let us make man"* and then Jesus acts upon the decision and makes man.

Getting back to Deuteronomy 6:4, it is evident that there is something more to this verse than meets the eye. *"Hear, O Israel: The LORD our God is one LORD."* [3]. If we take this verse the way it reads on the surface, we have a major problem, because in 1 Corinthians 8:6 we read: *"But to us there is but one God, the Father,*

---

1   Deuteronomy 6:4
2   Genesis 1:26
3   Genesis 1:27
4   Ephesians 3:9

of whom are all things, and we in him; and one Lord Jesus Christ, by whom are all things, and we by him." [1]

So we have one God and one Lord. But Deuteronomy said that God is only one Lord. This all sounds like a big play on words. Yet, the truth is simple and very profound.

The word "one" in Deuteronomy 6:4 is, echâd, which means "united":

"Properly united, that is, one; or (as an ordinal) first: a, alike, alone, altogether, and, any (-thing), apiece, a certain [dai-] ly, each (one), + eleven, every, few, first, + high-way, a man, once, one, only, other, some, together." [2]

Also taking into account that the word "God" used in this verse is the plural form, "'ĕlôhîym", it makes sense that God is trying to tell us that God is united as one.

In the context of this verse and in the proceeding verses, Moses is exhorting Israel to follow God and not the gods of the nations around them. One of the qualities that contrasts false gods from the True God is the fact the Godhead is perfectly united. All the other gods of human fabrication have wars and fight with each other. Unity amongst the leaders is the key to any stable government.

Some will argue that in most other cases where 'echâd is used, it is in the singular form. While that is true, it is the context that determines if it is singular or plural. Deuteronomy 6:4 connects 'echâd with the plural form of God ĕlôhîym, so it follows to reason that they both will be plural. Add to this the clear fact that Christ is also God, it becomes very clear what this verse is saying.

....

1   1 Corinthians 8:6
2   Strong's Greek Dictionary

In the Mouth of Two or Three Witnesses

One of the foundational principals in the Government of God is that for something to be confirmed as true, it must be verified by two or three witnesses.

"One witness shall not rise up against a man for any iniquity, or for any sin, in any sin that he sinneth: at the mouth of two witnesses, or at the mouth of three witnesses, shall the matter be established." [1]

Jesus also confirmed this principle in the New Testament:

"Moreover if thy brother shall trespass against thee, go and tell him his fault between thee and him alone: if he shall hear thee, thou hast gained thy brother. But if he will not hear thee, then take with thee one or two more, that in the mouth of two or three witnesses every word may be established." [2]

John applies this principle to Jesus when He died. There were three witnesses to confirm that Jesus was God: *"there are three that bear witness in earth, the Spirit, and the water, and the blood: and these three agree in one."* [3]

John is here referring to the Spirit that descended on Christ in the form a dove at His baptism, and the water and blood that flowed from His side when He was pierced on the cross.[4] These two instances John sights as witnesses to the authenticity of Jesus' Divinity.

This could be another reason why there are three persons in the Godhead. The only way that the Divinity of all three persons can be

1   Deuteronomy 19:15
2   Matthew 18:15,16
3   1 John 5:8
4   See John 1:32-34, and 19:33-37

confirmed is by the witness of two other witnesses. The Father's eternal presence is confirmed by Christ and the Holy Spirit. The eternal presence of Christ is confirmed by the Father and the Holy Spirit, and so on.

The 1 John 5:7 Controversy

There has been much controversy over the verse in 1 John 5:7 which says:

"For there are three that bear record in heaven, the Father, the Word, and the Holy Ghost: and these three are one." [1]

The only reason why there is controversy over this text is that it doesn't fit with the interpretations of some people, and there happened to be a few shady circumstances around this verse when it was translated. Christianity as a whole appears to fail to come to any agreement over this matter. Countless articles have been written, condemning and defending this one text.

It is not my intention to write yet another article trying to explain the history behind this text. The fact is, none of us were there, so none of us can know for sure.

But one thing is clear: This controversial text fits perfectly with the rest of scripture. Let me demonstrate. I will first quote the verse in its full context. Read it through slowly and carefully:

5:5 "Who is he that overcometh the world, but he that believeth that Jesus is the Son of God?
5:6 This is he that came by water and blood, even Jesus Christ; not by water only, but by water and blood. And it is the Spirit that beareth witness, because the Spirit is truth.
5:7 For there are three that bear record in heaven, the Fa-

....
1   1 John 5:7

*ther, the Word, and the Holy Ghost: and these three are
one.
5:8 And there are three that bear witness in earth, the Spirit,
and the water, and the blood: and these three agree in one.
5:9 If we receive the witness of men, the witness of God is
greater: for this is the witness of God which he hath testified
of his Son."* [1]

John is here gathering witnesses to prove that Jesus is indeed the
Son of God.

The Father witnessed that Jesus was His Son at His baptism, when
he declared publicly "this is my beloved Son". The Holy Spirit was
also present there.

Jesus Himself also declared Himself to be the Son of God. When
asked by the High Priest if He was the Son of God, replied: *"Thou
hast said: nevertheless I say unto you, Hereafter shall ye see the
Son of man sitting on the right hand of power, and coming in the
clouds of heaven."* [2]

When Peter was standing before the same counsel, after Jesus had
ascended to His Father, he said: *"The God of our fathers raised up
Jesus, whom ye slew and hanged on a tree. Him hath God exalted
with his right hand to be a Prince and a Saviour, for to give repentance to Israel, and forgiveness of sins. And **we are his witnesses
of these things**; **and so is also the Holy Ghost**, whom God hath
given to them that obey him."* [3]

So, the Father bears witness, Christ bears witness, and the Holy
Spirit bears witness. We can clearly see that 1 John 5:7 fits perfectly with the testimony of the rest of scripture. There is no need for
argument over this passage. God allowed this verse to find its way

....
1   1 John 5:5-9
2   Matthew 26:64
3   Acts 5:30-32

into the Bible, so let us leave it there!

The Only True God?

Another interesting interpretation which tries to throw a spanner in the works comes from John 17:3:

> *"And this is life eternal, that they might know thee the only true God, and Jesus Christ, whom thou hast sent."* [1]

This verse puzzled me for a time, because it seems to be saying that God the Father is the only true God and Jesus is secondary. This is a verse which the Jehovah's Witnesses often use to support their belief about Christ.

Is Jesus God? Yes indeed! We have covered this quite thoroughly in chapter two. The Father Himself declared this when He said to His Son, *"Thy throne, O God, is forever and ever: a sceptre of righteousness is the sceptre of thy kingdom."* [2]

Is John 17:3 a contradiction? No, not at all. Jesus is the only true God as well. In fact, in Isaiah 9:6 He is called *"The Mighty God"*.

Why then does Jesus seem to be excluding Himself, by addressing the Father as the only true God, and Himself as *"Jesus Christ, whom thou hast sent"*?

The light came on in my mind when I realised that Jesus is speaking as a man on earth. He was praying aloud in the hearing of many people. The only way to Salvation was through knowing God in heaven and Jesus Christ, who was right then down on earth with men. Jesus Christ who was sent is the man Jesus. The way of Salvation is knowing the man Jesus. It is how Jesus lived and walked

....

1   John 17:3
2   Hebrews 1:8

on earth. All these things show us the way of Salvation; how we are to act and live. This has nothing to do with excluding Jesus from the Godhead.

One God, The Father?

1 Corinthians 8:5,6 says,

> *"For though there be that are called gods, whether in heaven or in earth, (as there be gods many, and lords many,) But to us there is but one God, the Father, of whom are all things, and we in him; and one Lord Jesus Christ, by whom are all things, and we by him."* [1]

My initial comment is that this verse puts both the Father and Jesus as equal, because "Lord" refers to "God" as much as the word "God" itself. We also know that Jesus is God in the *"highest sense"* [2]

Why isn't the Holy Spirit mentioned here? Note that Paul is talking in the context of worship. The Bible says of the Holy Spirit that He does not speak of Himself. [3] The Holy Spirit's work is not to be worshiped and honoured as the God of earth. His work is behind the scenes, working to impress our hearts with the truth. He is the link between heaven and earth. This is why the Holy Spirit is not mentioned. Nowhere in the Bible do we find the command to worship the Holy Spirit on His own; to be worshiped is not His role.

The Great Commission

> *"Go ye therefore, and teach all nations, baptizing them in the name of the Father, and of the Son, and of the Holy Ghost."* [4]

....
1   1 Corinthians 8:5,6
2   1 Selected Messages p. 247
3   John 16:13
4   Matthew 28:19

This is one of the most powerful verses in the Bible. Yet it has been the cause of much controversy, because it strikes hard at some belief systems. When I carefully studied and contemplated this verse, the implications of this verse astounded me.

Jesus spoke these words just before He was about to leave His disciples and go to His Father. It is called the Great Commission, because that is exactly what it is: it is Jesus' commission to the disciples. But there is more to it than meets the eye. Let us consider the context:

"And Jesus came and spake unto them, saying, All power is given unto me in heaven and in earth." [1]

Here Jesus claims Divinity. He knew the Father had accepted His sacrifice and now all His power and authority that He had laid aside, had been returned to Him. Now He sent them forth in His power and authority, backed by the whole Godhead:

"Go ye therefore, and teach all nations, baptizing them in the name of the Father, and of the Son, and of the Holy Ghost." [2]

To baptise them in the name of the full Godhead meant that they had the full power and co-operation of the Godhead, working on their behalf to help them resist temptation. Ellen White says:

"When men and women, truly converted, are baptized in the name of the Father, Son, and Holy Ghost, these three representatives of heavenly authority behold the scene, and accept the vows made by human agents to walk henceforth in newness of life. In taking the baptismal vows, you have united with the highest powers in the heavenly courts, to live a life patterned after the life of Christ." [3]

....
1   Verse 18
2   Matthew 28:19
3   6 Manuscript Release p.29

This plainly shows that the Holy Spirit is just as much a living person as the Father and the Son. The Holy Spirit is one of the representatives of heavenly authority. He is not part of the Father and the Son, otherwise He would not be mentioned separately. Jesus goes on to say:

"Teaching them to observe all things whatsoever I have commanded you: and, lo, I am with you always, even unto the end of the world. Amen." [1]

The name of Jesus was the name by which the disciples preached, healed, and taught. It was in teaching everything that Jesus had told them and using His name that gave them the power.

When Anti-trinitarians are confronted with this verse, they will quickly point out that the Bible records the disciples as baptising "in the name of Jesus". Then they will make a list of possible reasons why. You will see something like this:

* The disciples were in direct disobedience to Jesus' command.
* Jesus didn't mean what He said.
* This verse does not belong in the Bible and was added later.
* The disciples understood Jesus command differently than we do.

This is a classic tactic which causes you to choose the answer they want you to choose because all the others cannot be true. But I would like to point out a fifth opinion:

* We don't actually know the exact words they used when they baptised people.

The Bible doesn't say that they said "I baptise you in the name of...." **However it was in the name of Jesus that people were converted**, because belief in Jesus as our personal Saviour is es-

1 Matthew 28:20

sential for salvation. The name of Jesus is the name of the God-head; *"For in him dwelleth all the fullness of the Godhead bodily."* [1] That is the emphasis of the book of Acts.

Using this scenario in Acts against a three person Godhead is setting up a straw man to divert from the real issue.

Ellen White's Description of The Godhead

In the midst of the Kellogg crisis Ellen White made a statement about the Godhead which clearly outlines the work of each person in the Godhead.

> *"The Father cannot be described by the things of earth. The Father is all the fullness of the Godhead bodily, and is invisible to mortal sight. The Son is all the fullness of the Godhead manifested. The word of God declares Him to be "the express image of His person." "God so loved the world that He gave His only begotten Son, that whosoever believeth in Him should not perish, but have everlasting life." Here is shown the personality of the Father.*
>
> *The Comforter that Christ promised to send after He ascended to heaven, is the Spirit in all the fullness of the Godhead, making manifest the power of divine grace to all who receive and believe in Christ as a personal Saviour. There are three living persons of the heavenly trio. In the name of these three powers,--the Father, the Son, and the Holy Ghost, those who receive Christ by living faith are baptized, and these powers will cooperate with the obedient subjects of heaven in their efforts to live the new life in Christ."* [1]

This is how Inspiration explains the Godhead. Three living persons, which include:

....
1   Bible Training School, March 1, 1906 par. 1,2; Evangelism p. 614, 615

The Father
* All the fullness of the Godhead bodily.
* Invisible from mortal sight.

The Son
* All the fullness of the Godhead manifested.
* Reveals the character of the Father.

The Holy Spirit
* All the fullness of the Godhead manifesting the power of divine grace.
* Reveals Christ.

Characteristics which all three have in common:
* Living persons.
* Have all the fullness of the Godhead.
* All have separate roles.

This last point is very important to consider in light of the many ideas that are floating around. Every member of the Godhead has a specific role. The Father is the head, the leader. Jesus Christ's work reveals the Father to us, by becoming a man, and walking on earth, showing what the Father is like. For eternity He holds that human body as a testimony to the love of God. The Holy Spirit's work is to complete the work of Christ on earth, now that Jesus is in heaven interceding on our behalf. The Holy Spirit reveals the grace of Christ to us, showing us what Christ's character is like.

The only way this beautiful plan can take place is when all three persons of the Godhead are living, individual persons. The fact that Jesus is not omnipresent means that the Holy Spirit must have a distinct, individual existence apart from Christ, otherwise Christ is still omnipresent, despite what the Bible and Ellen White say.

But the truth in its simplicity, is plain, yet deep and mind blowing at the same time. What an amazing and beautiful system God has for our Salvation! All we can say is, *"...let us consecrate to Him all that we are, and all that we have, and then may we all unite to swell the songs,--*

'Praise God, from whom all blessings flow;
Praise him, all creatures here below;
Praise him above, ye heavenly host;
Praise Father, Son, and Holy Ghost.'" [1]

Thus far in my journey, the Bible and Spirit of Prophecy have been in perfect harmony. Yet, there are still a few things that don't quite add up in my mind. So I set out to find out the truth of the matter. Join me in the next chapter, to tackle another challenging aspect of this topic.

....
1   Review and Herald, January 4, 1881 par. 18

Chapter 7

The Alpha and Omega of Deadly Heresies

The belief has been circulating in certain Adventist circles that the "omega of deadly heresies"—a phrase Ellen White coined and warned God's people about, is the doctrine of the Trinity—the belief that the Father, Son and Holy Spirit are three individual persons. Is this true? Did Ellen White really say that? What evidence is there to support this idea? What is the truth of the matter? These were the questions that I needed to solve. So I set out to find exactly where the truth of this matter lay. This is what I found.

The Historic Setting.

In order for us to understand the Alpha and Omega, we need to look at the historic setting where this term was born.

In the year 1904, Ellen White wrote: *"In the book Living Temple there is presented the alpha of deadly heresies. The omega will follow, and will be received by those who are not willing to heed the warning God has given."* [1]

It all started with a famous, well respected Adventist medical doctor by the name of Dr John Harvey Kellogg. Dr Kellogg came to believe that God was in nature—the trees, the flowers, the rocks, even in man himself—God was the life force that kept everything

1   Selected Messages, Vol. 1, p. 200

alive. This same idea is rampant in New Age philosophy. It made a concerted effort to make its way into the Seventh-day Adventist church through Dr Kellogg.

Yet these false ideas were conceived many years prior to its promulgation by Kellogg.

> *"Before the death of James White in 1881 J. H. Kellogg shared with the Whites some theories of 'new light' in understanding God. Ellen White responded forthrightly that she had 'met them before' and that he should 'never teach such theories in our institutions.'"* [1]

Despite the warnings from Sister White, in 1897 Kellogg shared his "new light" with the General Conference. His ideas were received well by those who were not grounded in the truth—*"What a wonderful thought, that this mighty God that keeps the whole universe in order, is in us! . . . What an amazing thing that this almighty, all-powerful, and all-wise God should make Himself a servant of man by giving man a free will—power to direct the energy within his body!"* [2] These were some of the thoughts expressed.

Then in the late 1890s E. J. Waggoner also picked up the same concepts.

At the 1899 General Conference, Kellogg presented many of his false ideas. He plainly taught that *"God is in everything."* [3]

Ellen White was in Australia at the time and was alerted by revelations from God as to what was happening in Battle Creek. She wrote letters, weeks prior to the 1899 General Conference, and they arrived right on time as the conference was starting. The first letter was called "The True Relation of God and Nature."—*"Na-*

1   Messenger of the Lord, Herbert E. Douglass, p. 200
2   General Conference Daily Bulletin Vol. 1, 1897, p. 83

ture is not God and never was God... As God's created work, it but bears a testimony of His power...We need carefully to consider this; for in their human wisdom, the wise men of the world, knowing not God, foolishly deify nature and the laws of nature." [1]

I must quickly add: what an incredible proof that Ellen White is inspired by God! No one knew weeks before, what Kellogg was going to say at the conference. But God did and He sent the revelation early, so it had time to travel half way around the world by ship, and arrive on time, to be read at the conference!

But this clear warning was disregarded by Kellogg and many of his supporters. A few years later in 1902, Dr Kellogg's world famous Battle Creek Sanitarium burned to the ground. This was a clear judgment from God.

Kellogg made plans at once to rebuild. He requested funds from the church. A. G. Daniells, the Conference president at the time, suggested he write a book on physiology and health care, which could be sold and used to raise money. But he warned Kellogg not

....
1   General Conference Daily Bulletin Vol. 8, 1899, p. 118

THINK ABOUT IT!

Kellogg's stubborn persistence in sticking to his beliefs, despite the judgments of God, are a warning to us. It is so easy to stick to our guns because we don't want to let go of our pride and surrender our pet ideas. I know I struggled with this in the beginning of my journey. It is hard to admit you are wrong.

But by God's grace we can give those feelings to God and look at the evidence objectively and ask, is the course I am following right or am I just trying to hold up my pride of opinion?

to include his theories about the nature of God. Kellogg at once began to write the book, which he entitled, *"The Living Temple"*.

A review of the book revealed that Kellogg did not listen to Daniells' warning. It included much of his pantheistic views about God. This created a great deal of controversy, and the General Conference Committee at last withdrew their support for the publication of the book. Kellogg then took out a personal order with the Review and Herald to get 5,000 copies of the book published. A month later the Review Publishing house burned to the ground. The plates for the book were destroyed in the fire. Ellen White was not surprised when she heard the news. Thirteen months before she had written:

"I have been almost afraid to open the Review, fearing to see that God has cleansed the publishing house by fire" [1]

Yet, despite this judgment from God, Kellogg got his book published by a commercial publisher.

It was with this background that Ellen White wrote to Dr Kellogg in 1903:

"You are not definitely clear on the personality of God, which is everything to us as a people. **You have virtually destroyed the Lord God Himself.***"* [2]

"Your ideas are so mystical that they are destructive to the real substance, and the minds of some are becoming confused in regard to the foundation of our faith. If you allow your mind to become thus diverted, you will give a wrong mold to the work that has made us what we are." [3]

....

1   Testimonies for the Church Vol 8, p. 91
2   Letter 300, 1903
3   Letter 52, 1903

"I am warned that we are not to talk of God as He is spoken of in Living Temple. The sentiments there expressed are a dishonor to His greatness and His majesty. God forbid that our ministers should entertain these ideas. For myself, I take my stand firmly against them. And I entreat you to accept the message that I bear to you. I ask you to arouse to your danger. Who by searching can find out God? **The theory that He is an essence, pervading everything, is one of Satan's most subtle devices.** *I warn you to beware of being led to accept theories leading to any such view. I tell you, my brother, that the most spiritual-minded Christians are liable to be deceived by these beautiful, seducing, flattering theories. But in the place of honouring God, these theories, in the minds of those who receive them, bring Him down to a low level, where He is nothingness."* [1]

"In Living Temple the assertion is made that God is in the flower, in the leaf, in the sinner. **But God does not live in the sinner.** *The Word declares that He abides only in the hearts of those who love Him and do righteousness. God does not abide in the heart of the sinner; it is the enemy who abides there."* [2]

"Scientific, spiritualistic sentiments, representing the Creator **as an essence pervading all nature** *have been given to our people, and have been received even by some who have had a long experience as teachers of the Word of God. The results of this insidious devising will break out again and again. There are many for whom special efforts will have to be put forth to free them from this specious deception."* [3]

....

1   Letter 230, 1903
2   Sermons and Talks, vol 1 p. 343
3   Battle Creek Letters, p. 79

*"The new theories in regard to God and Christ, as brought out in "The Living Temple", **are not in harmony with the teaching of Christ.** The Lord Jesus came to this world to represent the Father. He did not represent God as an essence pervading nature, but as a personal being. Christians should bear in mind that God has a personality as verily as has Christ."* [1]

Kellogg Revises the Living Temple

Kellogg received so much criticism from Ellen White and others that he decided to compromise. He shared his recantation with A. G. Daniells. Daniells later wrote a letter to Ellen White's son, W. C. White, outlining the outcome of this discussion:

"Ever since the council closed I have felt that I should write you confidentially regarding Dr Kellogg's plans for revising and republishing 'The Living Temple'... He said that some days before coming to the council, he had been thinking the matter over, and began to see that he had made a slight mistake in expressing his views. He said that all the way along he had been troubled to know how to state the character of God and his relation to his creation works... He then stated that his former views regarding the trinity had stood in his way of making a clear and absolutely correct statement; but that within a short time he had come to believe in the trinity and could now see pretty clearly where all the difficulty was, and believed that he could clear the matter up satisfactorily. He told me that he now believed in God the Father, God the Son, and God the Holy Ghost; and his view was that it was God the Holy Ghost, and not God the Father, that filled all space, and every living thing. He said if he had believed this before writing the book, he could have expressed his views without giving the wrong impression the book now gives.

....
1   Spalding and Magan Collection p. 324

I placed before him the objections I found in the teaching, and tried to show him that the teaching was so utterly contrary to the gospel that I did not see how it could be revised by changing a few expressions. We argued the matter at some length in a friendly way; but I felt sure that when we parted, the doctor did not understand himself, nor the character of his teaching. And I could not see how it would be possible for him to flop over, and in the course of a few days fix the books up so that it would be all right." [1]

Some Anti-trinitarians have used this letter to prove that Dr Kellogg accepted the Trinity doctrine which the Seventh-day Adventist church now holds to, and Ellen White and A. G. Daniells criticized him for it.

Yet, an objective reading of the letter, and Daniells' response to Kellogg shows that he understood the matter differently—*"I placed before him"*, Daniells said, *"the objections I found in the **teaching**, and tried to show him that the teaching was so utterly contrary to the gospel that I did not see how it could be revised by **changing a few expressions**."* Daniells recognised that Kellogg's new belief in the Trinity was simply *"changing a few expressions"* and that the real issue they were dealing with had not changed. Therefore the Trinity had nothing at all to do with the issue at stake.

Kellogg tried to explain his position in even clearer language to G.I. Butler in 1903:

*"As far as I can fathom, the difficulty which is found in 'The Living Temple', the whole thing may be simmered down to the question: **Is the Holy Ghost a person?** You say no. I had supposed the Bible said this for the reason that the personal pronoun 'he' is used in speaking of the Holy Ghost. Sister White uses the pronoun 'he' and has said in so many*

----

1   Letter: A. G. Daniells to W. C. White. October 29, 1903

words that the Holy Ghost is the third person of the God-head. How the Holy Ghost can be the third person and not be a person at all is difficult for me to see." [1]

Kellogg now tries to use Ellen White to back up his position. Again, some well-meaning people, including myself, have used this letter of Kellogg's to try and prove that the issue of the Holy Spirit being an individual person was one of Kellogg's errors. Yet, Kellogg himself denies this idea by explaining his use of the word "personality" in a letter to W. W. Prescott. I will quote from excerpts of that letter.

*"I believe this Spirit of God to be a personality, you don't. But this is purely a question of **definition**. I believe the Spirit of God is a personality; you say, No, it is not a personality. **Now the only reason why we differ is because we differ in our ideas as to what, a personality is.** Your idea of personality is perhaps that of semblance to a <u>person or a human being</u>. **<u>This is not the scientific conception of personality and that is not the sense in which I use the word</u>**. The scientific test for personality is the exercise, of will, volition, purpose, **without any reference to form or material being."** [2]*

Here Kellogg himself dismisses the idea that he believes the Holy Spirit to be a person by declaring that he is in agreement with Butler as to the personality of the Holy Spirit, but uses different terminology. He said that he believed the Holy Spirit is not a being with physical form, but a 'personality' capable of exercising *"will, volition, [and] purpose"*. This definition is rather confusing and vague. But later on in the same letter he stated his belief in the Holy Spirit in much clearer terms:

"You, Elder Daniells, and others have spoken about a fine line of distinction, but I could not quite see what it was, but

1   Letter: J. H. Kellogg to G. I. Butler, October 28, 1903
2   Letter: J. H. Kellogg to W. W. Prescott. October 25, 1903

*this statement by Sister White makes it clear to me. The difference is this: When we say God is in the tree, the word 'God' is understood in that the Godhead is in the tree, God the Father, God the Son, and God the Holy Spirit, whereas the proper understanding in order that wholesome conceptions should be preserved in our minds, is that God the Father sits upon his throne in heaven where God the Son is also; while **God's life, or Spirit or presence** is the all-pervading power which is carrying out the will of God in all the universe."* [1]

This is what Kellogg believed about the Holy Spirit. It is a far cry from the doctrine that the Bible and Ellen White teach, that the Holy Spirit is a distinct person. **In fact, Kellogg's understanding of the Holy Spirit fits quite well with the Anti-trinitarian belief of the Holy Spirit as the person and presence of God.**

"The Personality and Presence of God"

It is quite clear from our study so far, that the Omega of Deadly Heresies is not the Trinity doctrine. The issue is something different. Ellen White points out the real issue in the following quote:

*"I have been instructed by the heavenly messenger that some of the reasoning in the book Living Temple is unsound, and that this reasoning would lead astray the minds of those who are not thoroughly established on the foundation principles of present truth. It introduces that which is nought but speculation in regard to the **personality of God and where His presence is.** No one on this earth has a right to speculate on this question."* [2]

There are two key issues that Ellen White says are "but specula-

1 Ibid
2 Testimonies for the Church Containing Letters to Physicians and Ministers Instruction to Seventh-day Adventists p. 51

tion". They are Kellogg's understanding of:

1. The personality of God
2. Where His presence is

Kellogg clearly stated that he believed that:

> *"God the Father sits upon his throne in heaven where God the Son is also; while* **God's life, or Spirit or presence** *is the all-pervading power which is carrying out the will of God in all the universe."* [1]

Kellogg's understanding of the personality and presence of the Father and Christ is correct. Ellen White was very adamant that the Father and Christ sat on the throne in heaven. The problem lies in the nature of the Holy Spirit (Just as Kellogg said in his letter). The idea that the Holy Spirit is a power that pervades all nature was the error that Ellen White is addressing here.

In *Testimonies for the Church Containing Messages of Warning and Instruction to Seventh-day Adventists*, in an article entitled, *"Come Out and Be Separate"*, Ellen White clearly set forward the difference between Kellogg's false ideas and the truth:

> *"I am instructed to say, The sentiments of those who are searching for* *advanced scientific ideas are not to be trusted. Such representations as the following are made: "The Father is as the light invisible; the Son is as the light embodied; the Spirit is the light shed abroad." "The Father is like the dew, invisible vapor; the Son is like the dew gathered in beauteous form; the Spirit is like the dew fallen to the seat of life." Another representation: "The Father is like the invisible vapor; the Son is like the leaden cloud; the Spirit is rain fallen and working in refreshing power."*
>
> *"All these* *spiritualistic representations are simply noth-*

....
1   Letter: J H Kellogg to W. W. Prescott, Oct 25. 1903

*ingness. They are imperfect, untrue. They weaken and diminish the Majesty which no earthly likeness can be compared to. God cannot be compared with the things His hands have made. These are mere earthly things, suffering under the curse of God because of the sins of man. The Father cannot be described by the things of earth. **The Father is all the fullness of the Godhead bodily**, and is invisible to mortal sight."*

*"**The Son is all the fullness of the Godhead manifested.** The Word of God declares Him to be "the express image of His person." "God so loved the world, that He gave His only begotten Son, that whosoever believeth in Him should not perish, but have everlasting life." Here is shown the personality of the Father."*

*"The Comforter that Christ promised to send after He ascended to heaven, is **the Spirit in all the fullness of the Godhead, making manifest the power of divine grace** to all who receive and believe in Christ as a personal Saviour. **There are three living persons of the heavenly trio; in the name of these three great powers--the Father, the Son, and the Holy Spirit**-- those who receive Christ by living faith are baptized, and these powers will co-operate with the obedient subjects of heaven in their efforts to live the new life in Christ..."* [1]

Can you see the difference between Ellen White's explanation of the Godhead and Kellogg's? Note carefully the Holy Spirit. She said that the Holy Spirit is *"in all the fullness of the Godhead, making **manifest** the power of divine grace..."* The Holy Spirit manifests, or reveals the power of divine grace to us. This is a big difference. The Holy Spirit is not power of divine grace **itself**: He is a person that **reveals** that power to us. Just as Jesus manifested or revealed the Father, the Holy Spirit manifests or reveals Christ, through the wonderful grace that He has made available to us. This

....
1   Testimonies for the Church Containing Letters to Physicians and Ministers Instruction to Seventh-day Adventists p. 62, 63

reminds me of a quote we read in an earlier chapter:

"Of the Spirit Jesus said, "He shall glorify Me." The Saviour came to glorify the Father by the demonstration of His love; so the Spirit was to glorify Christ by revealing His grace to the world. The very image of God is to be reproduced in humanity. The honor of God, the honor of Christ, is involved in the perfection of the character of His people." [1]

The Holy Spirit reveals the grace of Christ to the world. He is not that grace; He is a person.

We conclude then that the issue God instructed Ellen White to face in Kellogg's teaching was his ideas regarding the personality and presence of the Holy Spirit. Initially, Kellogg believed that the whole Godhead was an impersonal force that filled all creation. After he was criticized he eventually changed his views and said it was the Holy Spirit that was God's power and life which filled all nature. Yet, Ellen White said he had not changed.

A superficial examination of Ellen White's writings, appears to reveal a striking similarity between them and Kellogg's writings. But there is a profound difference. Let us compare the two.

John Kellogg:
*"The manifestations of life are as varied as the different individual animals and plants, and parts of animated things. Every leaf, every blade of grass, every flower, every bird, even every insect, as well as every beast or every tree, bears witness to the infinite versatility and inexhaustible resources of the **one all-pervading,** all-creating, all-sustaining **Life.**"* [2]

Ellen White:

....
1   Desire of Ages p. 671
2   Living Temple p. 16

*"Not by its own inherent energy does the earth produce its bounties, and year by year continue its motion around the sun. An unseen hand guides the planets in their circuit of the heavens. **A mysterious life pervades all nature**--a life that sustains the unnumbered worlds throughout immensity, that lives in the insect atom which floats in the summer breeze, that wings the flight of the swallow and feeds the young ravens which cry, that brings the bud to blossom and the flower to fruit."* [1]

With just a surface reading of these two quotes it is little wonder people said that Kellogg's book contained the "very sentiments" Ellen White taught. But let's read a few more statements by Kellogg and see where the difference lies.

John Kellogg

*"God is the explanation of nature, not a God outside of nature, but **in nature**, manifesting himself through and in all the objects, movements, and varied phenomena of the universe... How can **power be separated** from the **source of power?** Where God's Spirit is at work, where God's power is manifested, God himself is actually and truly present."* [2]

*"Suppose now we have a boot before us,—not an ordinary boot, but a **living boot**, and as we look at it, we see little boots crowding out at the seams, pushing out at the toes, dropping off at the heels, and leaping out at the top,—scores, hundreds, thousands of boots, a swarm of boots continually issuing from our living boot,—would we not be compelled to say, "There is a shoemaker **in the boot**"? So there is present in the tree a power which creates and maintains it, **a tree-maker in the tree, a flower-maker in the flower**, . . . an infinite, divine, though invisible Presence . . . which is*

....

1   Education p. 99
2   Living Temple p. 28

ever declaring itself by its ceaseless, beneficent activity." [1]

Kellogg's mistake was this:

Kellogg confused the <u>power</u> of God with the <u>presence</u> of God.

His error was not in saying that the power of God is in nature. His error lay in linking that **power** with the **presence** of God, pulling God down to earth and placing Him in the trees and flowers, etc. God is a person. He is a real tangible being. The same applies to the Holy Spirit. The Holy Spirit cannot be God unless He is a real individual being.

The Holy Spirit does not pervade all nature. To say this would be to join Kellogg in his errors. The Holy Spirit is a person: the one who reveals and links the power of God to mankind. This is why Ellen White said,

> *"The Comforter that Christ promised to send after He ascended to heaven, is the Spirit in all the fullness of the God-head, **making manifest the power of divine grace** to all who receive and believe in Christ..." [2]*

The Holy Spirit is the channel through which the power of God flows to us.

> *"The work of the holy Spirit is immeasurably great. **It is from this <u>source</u> that power and efficiency come to the worker for God**; and the holy Spirit is the comforter, as the personal presence of Christ to the soul. He who looks to Christ in simple, childlike faith, is made a partaker of the divine nature through the agency of the holy Spirit." [3]*

....
1   Ibid. 29
2   Special Testimonies p. 63
3   Review and Herald, November 29, 1892 par. 3

*"In describing to His disciples the office work of the Holy Spirit, Jesus sought to inspire them with the joy and hope that inspired His own heart. He rejoiced because of the abundant help He had provided for His church. The Holy Spirit was the highest of all gifts that He could solicit from His Father for the exaltation of His people. The Spirit was to be given as a regenerating agent, and <u>without this the sacrifice of Christ would have been of no avail</u>. The power of evil had been strengthening for centuries, and the submission of men to this satanic captivity was amazing. <u>Sin could be resisted and overcome only</u> **through** <u>the mighty agency of the Third Person of the Godhead,</u> who would come with no modified energy, but in the fullness of divine power. It is the Spirit that makes **effectual** what has been wrought out by the world's Redeemer. It is by the Spirit that the heart is made pure. **Through the Spirit** the believer becomes a partaker of the divine nature. Christ has given His Spirit **as** a divine power to overcome all hereditary and cultivated tendencies to evil, and to impress His own character upon His church.* [1]

Do you see how it works? The reason why the work of the Holy Spirit is "immeasurably great" is because He is the link or the channel by which Christ comes in contact with us. Jesus has voluntarily laid aside His omnipresence, so this is the only way that He can be with us. We become partakers of the divine nature, through the Holy Spirit. Sin can only be resisted and overcome as we become connected with the power of God, through the Holy Spirit.

So we can conclude that Kellogg's view of the Godhead was wrong, not because he professed to believe in the Trinity, but because he confused the power of God with the presence of God. Ellen White maintained that the Holy Spirit was not a power pervading nature, but a distinct person.

....
1   Desire of Ages p. 671

It is not my intention to explore the many questions surrounding what the Omega of Deadly heresies are in this book. The purpose of this book is to reveal the truth about God, in the midst of the confusion and disagreement that surrounds it. I encourage you to study Ellen White's words on the Omega, and to do your own research, to pray and ask God to reveal to you what the Omega is so as to avoid being caught up in this deadly heresy. But I will give you a clue: it has to be something to do with spiritualism. Because the Alpha (Kellogg's view of God) was saying that God pervaded all nature and is in you (even the sinner). This is the foundation of spiritualism.

Thus far, I am convinced: There is total harmony in inspiration in regard to the nature of God. But there is one nagging problem that warrants investigation: it is the history of our church and the pioneers. Anti-trinitarians place a lot of emphasis on the pioneers and their teaching. Why? Join me in the next chapter to find out why, and to discover the truth behind all this.

Chapter 8

Our Pioneers
and the Doctrine of God

As I struggled to understand the truth about the Godhead, there was one thing that really puzzled me. Why did the pioneers of our faith have a different understanding of the Godhead than what the church has today? In fact, history tells us that the whole church once believed a different doctrine of the Godhead than what it presently taught. Is this an advance of truth or a slide back into error? I determined to understand this question, as it is needful that it be answered so that I could stand firm in my understanding of truth. Join me on a trip back into time to find out the truth of the matter.

"New Light" and the "Old Landmarks"

Ellen White speaks about the "Old Landmarks" which we must not move from. How does this relate to new light? Does it mean that there is no more room for a growth in knowledge and for new light to be brought to us? Listen to what Inspiration tells us:

> *"Men and women will arise professing to have some new light or some new revelation whose tendency is to **unsettle faith in the old landmarks**. Their doctrines will **not bear the test of God's word,** yet souls will be deceived. False reports will be circulated, and some will be taken in this snare."* [1]

....
1   Testimonies for the Church Vol 5 p. 295

So we need to be very careful about doctrines creeping into the church that take away the Old Landmarks. **The question is: What are the old landmarks?** In the book 1888 Messages, Ellen White clearly defines what the old landmarks are:

*"The passing of the **time in 1844** was a period of great events, opening to our astonished eyes the **cleansing of the sanctuary transpiring in heaven**, and having decided relation to God's people upon the earth, [also] **the first and second angels' messages and the third**, unfurling the banner on which was inscribed, "The commandments of God and the faith of Jesus." One of the landmarks under this message was the **temple of God, seen by His truth-loving people in heaven,** and the ark containing the law of God. The **light of the Sabbath of the fourth commandment flashed** its strong rays in the pathway of the transgressors of God's law. The **nonimmortality of the wicked is an old landmark. I can call to mind nothing more that can come under the head of the old landmarks. All this cry about changing the old landmarks is all imaginary."* [1]

Ellen White lists the following doctrines as the old landmarks.

1. 1844 and the cleansing of the sanctuary
2. The Three Angel's messages
3. The physical sanctuary in heaven
4. The Sabbath
5. The State of the Dead

These are the only landmarks that Ellen White under inspiration of God could recall. But I can think of many more that are foundational truths to Christianity. What about the Bible as the inspired word of God? What about salvation through Jesus Christ alone? What about the literal return of Christ the second time at the end of the earth? She did not mention any of these, because these are not

....
1   1888 Messages p. 518

landmark truths for Seventh-day Adventists.

At this point, an anti-trinitarian might disagree with the above statement and pull out Manuscript Release number 760 which says:

"Those who seek to remove the old landmarks are not holding fast; they are not remembering how they have received and heard. Those who try to bring in theories that would remove the pillars of our faith concerning the sanctuary or **concerning the personality of God or of Christ***, are working as blind men. They are seeking to bring in uncertainties and to set the people of God adrift without an anchor."* [1]

But they ignore the fact that the context of this quote is Kellogg and Ballenger's attempts at destroying the personality of God. The sanctuary message is based of the truth that God is a literal being and not a force in nature. This is what she is referring to. She is not saying that the Pioneer understanding of the Godhead is part of the pillars of our faith: But the fact that God is a literal person is.

What is a landmark? A landmark is a reference point which we can look at to know where we are going. So Ellen White is talking about distinctive doctrines that stand out: doctrines that separate the Seventh-day Adventist Church from the other churches from which it had come. Notice what Inspiration says:

"No line of our faith ___that has made us what we are___ *is to be weakened. We have the old landmarks of truth, experience, and duty, and we are to stand firm in defence of our principles, in full view of the world."* [2]

"He (Satan) seeks to create dissension, and to arouse contention and discussion, and to remove if possible the old

1   Manuscript Releases number 760 p. 9
2   Counsels on Health p. 521

*landmarks of truth **committed to God's people**. He tries to make it appear as if the Lord contradicts Himself."* [1]

*"Seventh-day Adventists have been chosen by God as **a peculiar people, separate from the world**. **By the great cleaver of truth He has cut them out from the quarry of the world** and brought them into connection with Himself.* [2]

What are these truths which set us, as Adventists, apart from the rest of the Christian world?

Without a doubt they are the landmarks that Ellen White listed in 1888 Messages p. 518. Read over them again and think about them. All of them are distinctive truths which separated us from the other churches. While is it true that a few churches have **some** of these doctrines, no other church has all of these truths. These truths are the rock solid foundation that our church was built on. If any of these are moved, the whole denomination will fall.

Is the Godhead part of the "Distinctive Truths"?

The next question that came to my mind after reading these quotes was, how does the Godhead doctrine fit into this? Was the Pioneer understanding of the Godhead part of these old landmarks setup by inspiration when our church was founded?

My research revealed that James White, Joseph Bates, Uriah Smith and other prominent leaders in the early advent movement came from the Christian Connection (or "Connexion") denomination, the first indigenous religious movement in America. This religious group were strong anti-trinitarians. *"But although the Bible is their only authoritative rule of faith and practice, yet the general characteristics of their belief may be determined. They are anti-trinitarians, yet call Christ a divine Saviour, and acknowledge the Holy*

---

1   Evangelism p. 359
2   Testimonies to the Church Vol. 7 p. 138

Spirit to be the power and energy of God" [1]

A review of the writings of the men from the Christian Connection reveals that their understanding of the Godhead was the same as that of the Pioneers. Below are a few statements from leading men in the Christian Connection compared with those of the Pioneers of the Seventh-day Adventist Church:

"The evidence we have to prove that ours is a divine Saviour is:
*1. Because he is God's son, in a peculiar sense **applicable to no other being in the universe.** In the scriptures angels and men are called sons of God, **but Christ is called his "own son," "his only-begotten son," "his beloved son,"** to distinguish him from others who are sons of God by creation, and regeneration..."* [2] *– James Williamson, Christian Connection.*

*"My own views of the Son of God, are, that he did not begin to exist 1820 years ago; **nor did he exist from eternity;** but was the **first begotten of the Father before time or creation began**--that he was sent by the Father 1820 years ago into the world, and united with a body, prepared for him; and that in him dwelt all the fullness of Godhead bodily..."* [3] *- Barton W. Stone, Christian Connection.*

*"This uncreated Word was the Being, who, in the fullness of time, was made flesh, and dwelt among us. His beginning was **not like that of any other being** in the universe. It is*

....

1   Philip Schaff, D.D., LL. D., A Religious Encyclopaedia: Or Dictionary Of Biblical, Historical, Doctrinal and Practical Theology, 1882, p. 449
2   The Religious Denominations in the United States: Their Past History, Present Condition, and Doctrines, 1859, p. 166
3   Barton W. Stone, Address to the Churches, p. 66

set forth in the mysterious expressions, ***"his [God's] only begotten Son"*** *(John 3:16; 1 John 4:9), "the only begotten of the Father" (John 1:14), and, "I proceeded forth and came from God." John 8:42."* [1] *– Uriah Smith, SDA Pioneer.*

*"It is true that there are many sons of God, but Christ is the "only begotten Son of God," and therefore the Son of God in a sense in **which no other being ever was or ever can be.** The angels are sons of God, as was Adam (Job 38:7; Luke 3:38), by creation; Christians are the sons of God by adoption (Rom. 8:14, 15), but Christ is the **Son of God by birth.**"* [2] *– E. J. Waggoner, SDA Pioneer.*

We can clearly see the similarity between the two views.

The pioneer understanding of the Godhead is not a distinctive truth to Adventists. **This doctrine, along with other doctrines such as Sunday worship, was carried into Adventism from the Chris-**

....

1   Uriah Smith, Looking Unto Jesus, p. 10
2   E. J. Waggoner, Christ and His Righteousness, p. 12

THINK ABOUT IT!

The main problem Ellen White had with Kellogg's understanding of the Godhead was that he made God into a nonentity. Instead of believing that God is a physical, tangible person, he taught that God was a spiritual power and presence. When Kellogg compromised His belief, he said that God the Father and Jesus Christ were individual persons, but that the Holy Spirit was God's "life", "Spirit" and "presence". But Ellen White insisted that Kellogg's underlying principle was still the same.

What does this tell us about the truth of the Holy Spirit? If the Holy Spirit was indeed the spirit and presence of God, Ellen White would have condoned him for accepting the truth. But instead, she strongly condemned him. This is proof that Ellen White believed that the Holy Spirit was an individual person.

tian denominations that they left. Should we then class this doctrine as one of the new and impacting truths that God gave to His people by Divine revelation? I cannot with a clear conscience do this. I believe it was all part of the growing process by which the light of truth became brighter and clearer through the Inspiration of the Holy Spirit.

How God Led His People

"The path of the just is as the shining light, that shineth more and more unto the perfect day." [1]

Our understanding of truth is often progressive. As God's people travel the path He has laid out for them, more truth is revealed. Old errors will be unlearned, and new light discovered. Time and history prove over and over again that this is God's chosen method of leading His people. He does not give all the light at once, but, like the dawning of a new day, the light of truth slowing but surely becomes brighter and brighter: until we can bask in the full glory of midday.

Let us take a look at the early history of our church and see if this pattern can be seen in the lives of our Pioneers.

From Sunday To Sabbath

Prior to 1846, Ellen White (Ellen Harmon at the time) and most of the Pioneers were still Sunday keepers. Joseph Bates was the one who introduced the Sabbath to the Advent Movement.

> *"Elder Bates was keeping the Sabbath, and urged its importance. Miss Harmon did not at that time feel its importance, and thought Elder Bates erred in dwelling upon the fourth commandment more than upon the other nine. But*

1 Proverbs 4:18

the Lord gave her a view of the heavenly sanctuary. The temple of God was opened in heaven, and she was shown the ark of God with the mercy-seat covering it. Two angels stood, one at either end of the ark, with their wings spread over the mercy-seat, and their faces turned toward it. This, her accompanying angel informed her, represented all the heavenly host looking with reverential awe toward the law of God which had been written by the finger of God. Jesus raised the cover of the ark, and she beheld the tables of stone on which the ten commandments were written. She was amazed as she saw the fourth commandment in the very centre of the ten precepts, with a soft halo of light encircling it. The angel said, "It is the only one of the ten which defines the living God who created the heavens and the earth and all things that are therein. When the foundations of the earth were laid, then was also laid the foundation of the Sabbath." She was shown that if the true Sabbath had been kept, there would never have been an infidel or an atheist. The observance of the Sabbath would have preserved the world from idolatry." [1]

From that point onward, the Sabbath was accepted by the early Adventists.

Health Reform

The Adventists also grew in their understanding of Health reform. James and Ellen White in the early days believed it was not a sin in eat pork.

"Before the health message came to Ellen White in 1863, she and James White both discouraged believers who attempted to enforce a prohibition on pork. "We do not, by any

---

1   J.N Loughborough, The Great Second Advent Movement, p. 255, 256

means, believe that the Bible teaches that its [pork] proper use, in the gospel dispensation, is sinful," James White
wrote in 1850." [1]

Yet, God lead Ellen White to understand the true light in regards to
health reform:

*"Over thirty years ago I was often in great weakness. Many
prayers were offered in my behalf. It was thought that flesh
meat would give me vitality, and this was, therefore, my principal article of diet. But instead of gaining strength, I grew
weaker and weaker. I often fainted from exhaustion. Light
came to me, showing me the injury men and women were
doing to the mental, moral, and physical faculties by the use
of flesh meat. I was shown that the whole human structure
is affected by this diet, that by it man strengthens the animal
propensities and the appetite for liquor." [2]*

Thus, one by one, the distinctive truths were laid down by revelations from God. Yet, the reforms did not all happen at once. Even
after the Seventh-day Adventist Church was officially established,
God had more light to give His people.

Righteousness by Faith

As the church grew, many of the Pioneers had an incorrect understanding of the Law of God and Righteousness by Faith. Their emphasis was too heavy on the Law, and many, Ellen White said, had
lost sight of Jesus as the one by whom Salvation comes. She said:

*"The Lord in His great mercy sent a most precious message
to His people through Elders Waggoner and Jones. This*

1   Ron Graybill, The Development of Adventist Thinking on Clean & Unclean Meats p. 1
2   Counsels on Diet and Foods p. 487

message was to bring more prominently before the world the uplifted Saviour, the sacrifice for the sins of the whole world. It presented justification through faith in the Surety; it invited the people to receive the righteousness of Christ, which is made manifest in obedience to all the commandments of God. Many had lost sight of Jesus. They needed to have their eyes directed to His divine person, His merits, and His changeless love for the human family. All power is given into His hands, that He may dispense rich gifts unto men, imparting the priceless gift of His own righteousness to the helpless human agent. This is the message that God commanded to be given to the world. It is the third angel's message, which is to be proclaimed with a loud voice, and attended with the outpouring of His Spirit in a large measure." [1]

"I have had the question asked, what do you think of this light which these men [A. T. Jones and E. J. Waggoner] are presenting? Why, I have been presenting it to you for the last forty-five years,--the matchless charms of Christ. This is what I have been trying to present before your minds." [2]

God sent the message of Righteousness by Faith to awaken the people and bring them onto a higher plane of truth.

The Doctrine of God

If the church's doctrines were growing and expanding, it is quite appropriate to expect the doctrine of the nature of God to also grow as God revealed more light. We saw in an earlier section that the Pioneer understanding on the nature of God came from other Christian denominations, so we would expect a change would have to come about as the church grew in Biblical understanding in this area also.

1   Testimonies to Ministers p. 91
2   Manuscript 5, 1889, p. 10. [Sermon delivered at Rome, N. Y., June 17, 1889.]

For example, in 1865, Uriah Smith wrote in his book, Thoughts Critical and Practical on the book of Revelation:

*"Moreover he is "the beginning of the creation of God." Not the beginner, but the beginning, of the creation, **the first created being**, dating his existence far back before any other created being or thing, next to the self-existent and eternal God. On this expression Barnes makes the following significant admission: "if it were demonstrated from other sources that Christ was, in fact, **a created being**, and the first that God had made, it cannot be denied that this language would appropriately express that fact."* [1]

Clearly, Uriah Smith believed that Jesus was a created being. However in the 1882 edition of the same book he shows a change in His ideas:

*"Others, however, and more properly we think, take the word to mean "agent" or "efficient cause," which is one of the definitions of the word, understanding that Christ is the agent through whom God has created all things, **but that he himself came into existence in a different manner**, as he is called "the only begotten" of the Father. It would seem utterly inappropriate to apply this expression to any being created in the ordinary sense of the term."* [2]

Smith also believed that the Holy Spirit was not an individual person:

"But respecting this Spirit, the Bible uses expressions which cannot be harmonized with the idea that it is a person like

....
1   Thoughts Critical and Practical on the book of Revelation, p. 59
2   Thoughts on the Book of Daniel and the Revelation p. 487

the Father and the Son. Rather it is shown to be a divine influence from them both, the medium which represents their presence and by which they have knowledge and power through all the universe, when not personally present." [1]

The Pioneers hotly contested the idea of Christ being eternal with the Father.

"The idea of the Father and Son supposes priority of the existence of the one, and the subsequent existence of the other. To say that the Son is as old as the Father, is a palpable contradiction of terms. It is a natural impossibility for the Father to be as young as the Son, or the Son to be as old as the Father." [2]

J. M. Stephenson also clearly believed that Jesus was a created being:

"Col. 1:15. "the first born of every creature." Creature signifies creation; hence to be the first born of every creature, (creation) **he must be a created being***; and as such,* **his life and immortality must depend upon the Father's will just as much as angels, or redeemed man...."* [3]

What was the Early Church's Official Position on the Godhead?

As an Anti-trinitarian, I always believed that the Church officially upheld the Pioneer understanding of the Godhead. But searching into the history of our church, it became clear that things were not as clear cut as what I was led to believe. In fact there was no real official position on the Godhead until 1931 when F. M. Wilcox draft-

1   "In the Question Chair," Review and Herald, October 28, 1890
2   J. M. Stephenson, "The Atonement," Review and Herald, VI (Nov 14, 1854), 128.
3   Ibid.

ed the first statement of beliefs.

Uriah Smith wrote a document called *"A Declaration of the Fundamental Principles Taught and Practiced by the Seventh-day Adventists"* which outlines the beliefs held by the Seventh-day Adventist Movement at the time. What did it say? Here is the first few paragraphs:

"In presenting to the public this synopsis of our faith, we wish to have it distinctly understood that we have no articles of faith, creed, or discipline, aside from the Bible. We do not put forth this as having any authority with our people, nor is it designed to secure uniformity among them, as a system of faith, but is a brief statement of what is, and has been, with great unanimity, held by them...

With these remarks, we ask the attention of the reader to the following propositions, which aim to be a concise statement of the more prominent features of our faith.

That there is one God, a personal, spiritual being, the creator of all things, omnipotent, omniscient, and eternal, infinite in wisdom, holiness, justice, goodness, truth, and mercy; unchangeable, and everywhere present by his representative, the Holy Spirit. Ps. 139:7.

That there is one Lord Jesus Christ, the Son of the Eternal Father, the one by whom God created all things, and by whom they do consist; that he took on him the nature of the seed of Abraham for the redemption of our fallen race; that he dwelt among men full of grace and truth, lived our example, died our sacrifice, was raised for our justification, ascended on high to be our only mediator in the sanctuary in Heaven, where, with his own blood he makes atonement for our sins; which atonement so far from being made on the cross, which was but the offering of the sacrifice, is the very last portion of his work as priest according to the example of the Levitical priesthood, which foreshadowed and prefigured the ministry of our Lord in Heaven." [1]

This declaration of the church's position of the Godhead is very ambiguous and raises more questions then it answers. There is a lot of room in this statement for a wide range of interpretations. In fact, there is nothing in there that our current church statement of beliefs would disagree with. Nothing is said of Christ's divinity, or of the nature of the Holy Spirit.

Ellen White's Understanding of the Godhead

Some people cringe at the suggestion that Ellen White's understanding of the Godhead could have been wrong at one point. Yet, if her understanding of the Sabbath and health reform were wrong at one point, it seems likely that she would have incorrect ideas concerning the Godhead at one point as well. God inspired her to write the books and articles we have today, and God did not allow her to write something that was wrong. However, as we will see, her understanding regarding the Godhead was progressive as was her understanding of other areas of doctrine. This is to be expected.

Ellen White came from a Trinitarian Methodist background which believed in a more Catholic style Trinity, three persons in one substance:

*"There is but one living and true God, everlasting, **without body or parts,** of infinite power, wisdom, and goodness; the Maker and Preserver of all things, both visible and invisible. And in unity of this Godhead there are three persons, of one substance, power, and eternity—the Father, the Son,*

....
1   A Declaration of The Fundamental Principles Taught And Practiced by the Seventh-Day Adventists, Published 1872.

and the Holy Ghost." [1]

This is clearly the Trinity doctrine that the Pioneers strongly opposed.

Joseph Bates:
*"Respecting the trinity, I concluded that it was an impossibility for me to believe that the Lord Jesus Christ, the Son of the Father, was also the Almighty God, the Father, **one and the same being.**"* [2]

James White:
*"Jesus prayed that his disciples might be one as he was one with his Father. This prayer did not contemplate one disciple with twelve heads, but twelve disciples, made one in object and effort in the cause of their master. Neither are the Father and the Son **parts of the "three-one God." They are two distinct beings,** yet one in the design and accomplishment of redemption."* [3]

A. J. Denis:
*"What a contradiction of terms is found in the language of Trinitarian creed: "In unity of this head are three persons, of **one substance**, power, and eternity, the Father, the Son, and the Holy Ghost." There are many things that are mysterious, written in the word of God, but we may safely resume the Lord never calls upon us to believe impossibilities. But creeds often do.* [1]

....
1   Official text of the Articles of Religion, United Methodist Church Website, viewed January 2018, http://www.ccel.org/ccel/schaff/creeds3.v.vi.html
2   Joseph Bates, 1868, The Autobiography Of Elder Joseph Bates, page 204
3   James White, 1868, Life Incidents, page 343

Ellen White in her early writings took up the same tenor as her collaborates, though in an indirect manner. She emphasized the fact that the Father and Son are distinct persons, not spiritual manifestations.

"I have often seen the lovely Jesus, that he is a person. I asked him if his Father was a person, and had a form like himself. Said Jesus, "I am in the express image of my Father's Person." I have often seen that the spiritual view took away the glory of heaven, and that in many minds the throne of David, and the lovely person of Jesus had been burned up in the fire of spiritualism." [1]

She continued to teach this truth throughout her life. In 1905 she wrote:

*"In this Scripture God and Christ are spoken of as **two distinct personalities**, each acting in their own individuality."* [2]

But in 1893 she had written that the Holy Spirit is also a distinct personality:

*"The Holy Spirit is the Comforter, in Christ's name. He personifies Christ, yet is a **distinct personality**. We may have the Holy Spirit if we ask for it and make it [a] habit to turn to and trust in God rather than in any finite human agent who may make mistakes.* [3]

In 1906 she stated her understanding of the Holy Spirit in even clearer language:

....

1   Spiritual Gifts Vol. 2, p. 74
2   Manuscript Release No. 760, p. 18, 1905
3   Manuscript Release Vol 20, p. 324, 1893

*"The Holy Spirit **has a personality**, else He could not bear witness to our spirits and with our spirits that we are the children of God. He must also be a **divine person**, else He could not search out the secrets which lie hidden in the mind of God. "For what man knoweth the things of a man save the spirit of man, which is in him; even so the things of God knoweth no man, but the Spirit of God."* [1]

To the Students at Avondale College she said:

*"We have been brought together as a school, and we need to realize that the Holy Spirit, who is as **much a person as God is a person**, is walking through these grounds, that the Lord God is our keeper, and helper. He hears every word we utter and knows every thought of the mind."* [2]

Here Ellen White makes no distinction between the Holy Spirit and the Father. "Just as much a person" means just that. You cannot believe that the Holy Spirit is part of the Father, and say something like that.

Ellen White confirmed the Divinity of the Holy Spirit in Desire of Ages:

*"Sin could be resisted and overcome only through the mighty agency of the **Third Person of the Godhead**, who would come with no modified energy, but in the fullness of divine power."* [3]

Ellen White's understanding of the Divinity of Christ also grew in clarity and strength. For example:

....
1   Manuscript 20, 1906, Evangelism p. 617
2   Manuscript 66, 1899, p. 4. (Talk, April 15, 1899)
3   Desire of Ages p. 671

"The great Creator assembled the heavenly host, that he might in the presence of all the angels confer special honor upon his Son. The Son was seated on the throne with the Father, and the heavenly throng of holy angels was gathered around them. The Father then made known that it was ordained by himself that Christ, his Son, should be equal with himself; so that wherever was the presence of his Son, it was as his own presence. The word of the Son was to be obeyed as readily as the word of the Father. His Son he had invested with authority to command the heavenly host." [1]

Reading this on its own, one could easily come to the understanding that Christ was then raised to the level of Divinity by the Father. But, in 1890, when the book was republished as Patriarchs and Prophets, Ellen White clarified the statement:

"There had been no change in the position or authority of Christ. Lucifer's envy and misrepresentation and his claims to equality with Christ had made necessary a statement of the true position of the Son of God; **but this had been the same from the beginning.** *Many of the angels were, however, blinded by Lucifer's deceptions."* [2]

Ellen White followed this statement with an even clearer cutting statement regarding the Divinity and eternal presence of Christ:

"With solemn dignity Jesus answered, "Verily, verily, I say unto you, Before Abraham was, I AM."

Silence fell upon the vast assembly. The name of God, given to Moses to express the idea of the eternal presence, had been claimed as His own by this Galilean Rabbi. He had announced Himself to be the **self-existent One**, *He who had been promised to Israel, "whose goings forth have*

....
1   Spirit of Prophecy Vol. 1 p.17
2   Patriarchs and Prophets p. 38

been from of old, from the days of eternity." Micah 5:2, margin." [1]

"Christs is the **pre-existent, self-existent** Son of God.... In speaking of his pre-existence, Christ carries the mind back **through dateless ages**. He assures us that there **never was a time** when He was not in close fellowship with the eternal God. He to whose voice the Jews were then listening had been with God as one brought up with Him." [2]

(Revelation 1:18-20 quoted.) "These are wonderfully solemn and significant statements. It was the **Source of all** mercy and pardon, peace and grace, the **self-existent, eternal, unchangeable** One, who visited His exiled servant on the isle that is called Patmos." [3]

"I am the resurrection, and the life." In Christ is life, **original, unborrowed, underived.** "He that hath the Son hath life." 1 John 5:12. The divinity of Christ is the believer's assurance of eternal life." [4]

"Before the mountains were brought forth, or ever thou hadst formed the earth and the world, even from everlasting to everlasting, thou art God" (Psalm 90:2). "The people which sat in darkness saw great light; and to them which sat in the region and shadow of death light is sprung up" (Matthew 4:16). **Here the preexistence of Christ** and the purpose of His manifestation to our world are presented as living beams of light from the eternal throne. "Now gather thyself in troops, O daughter of troops: he hath laid siege against us: they shall smite the judge of Israel with a rod upon the cheek. But thou, Bethlehem Ephratah, though

....

1   Desire of Ages p. 469
2   Signs of the Times, Aug. 29, 1900
3   Manuscript 81, 1900, Bible Commentary Vol 7, p. 955
4   Desire of Ages p. 530

*thou be little among the thousands of Judah, yet out of thee shall he come forth unto me that is to be ruler in Israel; whose goings forth have been from of old, **from everlasting**" (Micah 5:1, 2).* [1]

With such clear cut statements as these, in contrast with her earlier statements, and those of her co-workers, there is little doubt that Ellen White's understanding of the Godhead developed as God revealed more light to her. If God had given her all those clear, hard hitting statements in the early days, it would have created much division in the church, and shaken the confidence of the early Adventists in the prophetic gift of Ellen White. So God waited until

....
1   1 Selected Messages p. 248, 1906

APPLY IT TO YOUR LIFE!

It should be no surprise that the Pioneers grew in their knowledge, understanding and experience. When you first discovered the truth, did you have it all right to begin with? Not usually! God never floods us with all the light and knowledge there is to know. If He did, it would overwhelm us! It's like a child learning to read. You don't hand him a university level science text book as His first reader do you? No, of course not! Why not? Because he cannot handle all that knowledge. He won't understand it. Neither does he have the tools to understand it. So we have to give him a simplified book to read first, and once he can read that, then we can give him more complex things to understand.

It is the same with God. He does not give us everything at once. He gives us light and truth as our minds can grasp it. He did that for the Pioneers, and He does it with us today. But we have had more opportunities then the Pioneers did. We have access to Ellen White's writings like no one has had before. With the advent of computers and fast printing presses, we can have a wealth of information before us. We have no excuse not to know the truth. Let us then study the truth like never before and ask God to reveal the light to us, as our minds expand with study and prayer.

other, clearer truths were established.

Evidence of a Change in Thinking

There is good evidence to show that there was a clear change in Adventist thinking regarding the Godhead in the late 1800s and early 1900s. In 1892, the Pacific Press published an article by Presbyterian minister named the Rev. Samuel Spear D.D. The article was called "The Bible doctrine of the Trinity" [1]. In this article he referred to the three persons of the Godhead has "God the Father, God the Son and God the Holy Ghost.

In 1901, H. F. Phelps published an article in the Review and Herald called "When Was God's Eternal Purpose Revealed?" Here's what he said:

*"But now let the mind enlarge to take in some of the eternity of the past. There must have been a beginning of this revelation, a beginning of the work of creation. And this must have been the very beginning of the revelation of that same eternal purpose. Preceding this beginning, there must have been, according to Rom. 16: 25, R. V., " times eternal," when there were no worlds, no created being, not even an angel; in fact, **there were only three beings—God the Father, God the Son, and God the Holy Spirit ; these three persons in the Godhead.**" [2]*

And there here's a few more statements from our church publications that clearly show a change in their thinking:

"Let us not grow overbold concerning the Spirit alone; but remember that he is ever with the Father and the Son, and that whatever he speaks to us he speaks as from them; for

1   Student Bible Series, No. 90, The Bible doctrine of the Trinity, Pacific Press, 1892
2   H.F. Phelps, Review and Herald, Vol. 78, No. 1, January 1, 1901
    http://documents.adventistarchives.org/Periodicals/RH/RH19010101-V78-01.pdf

it is written, "Whatsoever he shall hear, that shall he speak."
Let him make you know, beloved, how surpassingly beauti-
*ful are the **blended personalities of our <u>triune God</u>, man-***
ifested by the personal presence of the Holy Ghost. *" 1*
"...in the formula for baptism, the name "Holy Ghost," or"
Holy Spirit," is associated with that of the Father and the
Son. And if the name can be used thus, why could it not
*properly stand as a part of the same **Trinity in the hymn of***
praise, "Praise Father, Son and Holy Ghost"? *" 2*

"Gabriel was only an angel, upheld by the same Power that
sustained John, and he would not for one moment allow
*John to be deceived by thinking he was a **part of the great***
***Trinity of heaven,** and worthy of the worship of mankind." 3*

"What a picture is this! **The Father, the Son, and the Holy**
Spirit three divine comforters—pledged to every soul
who will yield himself to the messages of infinite love! Who
needs to go groping his way in sadness and gloom? The
great Captain of our salvation said, 'I will not leave you com-
fortless.' Then lift your heads, ye sorrowing, mourning ones,
and listen to the blessed words of comfort which are given
in the divine Word." 4

This next quote by R. A. Underwood, shows how he changed his
view on the Holy Spirit:

"It was once hard for me to see how a spirit could be a
person; but when I saw "that God is a spirit" (John &: 24),
and that he is no less a person; when I saw that the last
Adam (Christ) "was made a quickening spirit" (1 Cor. 15 :

1   Review and Herald April 3, 1900 p. 2 "Blended Personalities"
    http://documents.adventistarchives.org/Periodicals/RH/RH19000403-V77-14.pdf
2   Uriah Smith, Review and Herald, 1896, Vol. 73, No. 43, pg. 685
3   S.N. Haskell, The Story of Daniel the Prophet, 1905 edition, pg. 132
4   D. A. Robinson, Review and Herald, December 28, 1897
    http://documents.adventistarchives.org/Periodicals/RH/RH18971228-V74-52.pdf

45), and that he is a person; when I saw that the angels are "spirits" (Heb. 1 : 7, 14), and even that the fallen angels, called "devils" are said to be "unclean spirits" (Luke 8 : 26, 29; Acts 19:15, 16); and knowing that all these are persons, **I could understand better how the Holy Spirit can be a person.** ... Christ has put into the field, as **his personal representative, the Holy Ghost**, who is in charge of all the forces of God's kingdom to overthrow Satan and his angels; and the Holy Ghost is the only one to whom is delegated this authority from God. "The prince of the power of evil can be held in check only by the power of God in the third person of the Godhead, the Holy Spirit."—"Special Testimony," No. 10, page 37. God and Christ have placed all the angels and the power of the throne of omnipotence under him [the Holy Spirit], to overthrow the rebellion against God's government.... **The Holy Ghost being Christ's representative, and Christ being the Father's representative, the Holy Ghost represents both the Son and the Father; and the work done by the Holy Spirit is accredited to those whom he represents, for he is their agent.** Again: the Holy Spirit being in charge of all the holy angels, whatever is done by them under the authority of the Holy Spirit, is accredited the work of the Holy Spirit." [1]

So without a doubt, the change in Adventist thinking happened much earlier then the anti-trinitarians would like us to believe.

Why No Clear Statement Regarding the Change?

It has been asked, "Why didn't God send Ellen White a clear message to the church saying, here is new light regarding the Godhead?" We need to remember that the church had no official position on the finer details of the Godhead. Different people had slightly different ideas regarding God, but they all believed the basics, just

1   R.A. Underwood, "The Holy Spirit a Person", Review & Herald, May 17, 1898, pg. 310
    http://documents.adventistarchives.org/Periodicals/RH/RH18980517-V75-20.pdf

like we do today: That there is the Father, Jesus Christ and the Holy Spirit who is Christ's representative. That knowledge was all that was needed at that time. In fact, they could have been translated with that knowledge, because Ellen White is clear in Early Writings that Jesus was ready to come within a few short years of 1844.

But as time dragged on because of the slowness of God's people, more false ideas about God started to arise. God then saw fit to give more light regarding Himself. This is clear when you consider that around 1897 Dr Kellogg started to come out publicly with his false theories about God. And it was around 1897 onwards that we see Ellen White emphasizing that there are three persons in the Godhead and that the Holy Spirit is a person. Take a look at these phrases from Ellen White:

*   *"The Holy Spirit is a person..."* [1] *-1906*
*   *"Three living persons of the heavenly trio"* [2] *- 1905*
*   *"Three highest powers in heaven..."* [3] *- 1905*
*   *"The eternal heavenly dignitaries..."* [4] *- 1901*
*   *"The Godhead was stirred with pity for the race..."* [5] *- 1901*
*   The Holy Spirit is *"as much a person as God is a person"* [6] *- 1899*
*   *"The third person of the Godhead..."* [7] *- 1897*
*   *"The Holy Spirit...is a distinct personality"* [8] *- 1893*

If you study the context of some of the above statements, you will find that Ellen White is combating Kellogg's false ideas. So clearly, God saw that more information was needed to dispel this erroneous view of God. In this sense, there was no "official change"

....

1   Manuscript 20, 1906, Manuscript Releases Vol. 20 p. 69
2   Evangelism p. 615, Testimonies for the Church Containing Messages of Warning and Instruction to Seventh-day Adventists p. 63
3   Evangelism p. 617, Testimonies for the Church Containing Messages of Warning and Instruction to Seventh-day Adventists p. 51
4   Evangelism p. 616, Manuscript Releases Vol. 16, p. 205
5   Review and Herald May 2, 1912, par. 3
6   Evangelism p. 616, Sermons and Talks Vol. 2, p. 136
7   Desire of Ages p. 671
8   Manuscript Releases Vol. 20, p. 324

because they never had an official position. What we see is an advancement in knowledge.

Instead of ignoring the facts and clinging to our own ideas, let us accept the truth that God has brought to us through inspiration. There is much truth in the line from the old hymn, *Once to Every Man and Nation*, which says, *"They must upward still and onward, who would keep abreast of truth"*. [1]

---

1   James Russell Lowell, Seventh-day Adventist Hymnal number 606

Chapter 9

From Confusion to Conclusion!

This brings us to the conclusion of our journey. We started with the nature of Christ, and the question of His Divinity. This has taken us right back to the beginning of time and beyond. We have explored the Bible and the Spirit of Prophecy. We have turned back the pages of our denominational history, and searched the archives to discover the lives and letters of our Pioneers. My study has lead me to an inescapable conclusion: My former position on the nature of God is error and I must renounce it. Here are my reasons in summary:

Why I Left the Anti-trinitarian Movement

- **Belief in this doctrine casts doubt on Inspiration.** There are many Spirit of Prophecy quotes and some Bible verses which don't agree with what Anti-trinitarians teach. Consequently they are forced to claim that copyists made mistakes, biased leaders changed statements they didn't agree with, and Ellen White herself, in her wording, has made plain truths confusing. I have seen people start on this path, which has led them to totally reject Ellen White, and even parts of the Bible.

- **This doctrine robs Christ of His eternal existence.** The teaching of this doctrine uses human explanations to explain divine truths which are not fully revealed to us. People reason that in order for Christ to be the Son of God, He must be a literal son in the biological sense. Where is the Biblical authority for such a claim? There is only one time, according to the Bible, when Christ was born, and that was in Bethlehem. If Christ came into existence, what stops us from going to the next step by saying that He could cease to exist? Ellen White tells us this is impossible. [1]

- **It lies very close to other false religions.** The idea that Christ came into existence is a doctrine which the Jehovah's Witnesses hold to. They take the next step and say that Christ was created. But is there really any difference between that and what many Anti-trinitarians believe? No one has been able to give me a tangible difference. Remember, God does not procreate like we do. He speaks, and things come into being. That is creation.

- **It casts mystery over the simple concept of eternity.** Once I came to believe in this doctrine, eternity ceased to be eternity. It was a mystery that could not be explained. Someone can be eternal, and yet have a beginning. There is no such Biblical proof for this idea, it is completely of human origin. If people must resort to such theories to maintain their position, that alone is enough to call into question the whole truth of the doctrine. Every teaching must have a clear "Thus saith the Lord".

- **It brings into question the greatness of the sacrifice of God in becoming Man, and the whole concept of the Plan of Redemption.** There are several ways that it does this:

  1. Instead of God Himself coming to die, He sends His Son. Why did He not go Himself?

....
1   *See 5 Bible Commentary p. 1113*

2. **This doctrine teaches that God could not die, therefore He had to send His Son.** Right away, this idea hints that Christ is less Divine than the Father. Secondly, it is humanity trying to find a solution for a problem which we were never meant to solve. We need to simply accept the Bible as it reads and believe it.

3. **It makes a mockery of Christ sending the Comforter.** If the Holy Spirit is Christ in another form, then Christ is still omnipresent, despite the fact that inspiration plainly says Christ did lay down His omnipresence. It also makes Christ's words meaningless when He promised to send "another comforter" who would "testify" of Him.

4. **Instead of an eternal bond between the Father and Son being broken up,** this doctrine teaches that Christ's bond with the Father is not eternal and had a beginning.

• **It rests its teachings on principles that are not clearly stated in the Bible.** Anti-trinitarians believe that Christ was birthed by the Father in eternity past, when there is not one scripture verse that says so. The only time when we read about Christ being born is in Bethlehem.

• **Those who uphold this theory must take Bible texts and Ellen White quotes out of context to support their beliefs.** As I have examined the so called "proof texts" for Anti-trinitarianism, I have had to admit on each and every occasion, they were out of context and twisted to suit the agenda of the proponents of this doctrine.

What matters most...

At the end of the day, despite all the evidence that we have seen in the Bible and Spirit of Prophecy, we really don't know what we are talking about. God reveals enough about Himself for us to grasp what is important about Him. But God remains a mystery to us. When we start trying to figure out what God has not revealed, that's when we get into trouble. As we saw earlier, the nature of the Holy Spirit is not clearly revealed and sometimes silence is golden. What's important is this: that we focus on what is clearly revealed in scripture. Many people that get caught up in the Anti-trinitarian movement make this topic the all-important test for the people of God. But this is a dangerous idea. Because it's not clearly revealed, there are many interpretations and who is to know which interpretation is right? We are best to just read what God has revealed, accept it and believe it, without adding any speculation to it. Then we must be content to accept the parts that we don't understand and leave them to God, who will reveal them to us in His own time, after sin is forever dealt with.

So please, don't spend the rest of your life studying the Godhead. I have written this book because I was very confused over this issue and I wanted to share with people how God led me. But I don't want this issue to become our focus. The very fact that God hasn't clearly revealed some areas of Himself should tell us that it's not needful that we understand them. Let's move our focus on to the great truths of salvation and prepare ourselves for Jesus' soon coming. Rather than debating about who the Holy Spirit is, let's open our hearts to Him and allow Him to do that transforming work in us, so we can all go home. Then the many questions that haven't been answered this side of heaven will be made plain.

There is nothing Satan wants more but to divert us from what is most important. He has used the Godhead debate to do this very successfully. I have seen it happen many times.

So, dear reader, I challenge you to carefully and prayerfully consider the points I have raised in this book. I pray that it has been helpful to you and will inspire you to study more. Most of all, I hope it has given you a greater insight into the love of God and His incredible plan to save humanity. May this be our focus and not the fine details of the Godhead. That's what matters most.

"The grace of the Lord Jesus Christ, and the love of God, and the communion of the Holy Ghost, be with you all. Amen." [1]

....
1 1 Corinthians 13:14

Appendix A

Photocopies of Ellen White's Manuscripts

There are many conspiracies circulating regarding Ellen White's statements that clearly uphold a three distinct person Godhead. Were these statements doctored by the church to make Ellen White say something she never said? Look at the evidence and make up your own mind. All these photocopies come from the Ellen White Estate website. [1]

"Three Living Persons of the Heavenly Trio"

*"There are **three living persons of the heavenly trio; in the name of these three great powers—the Father, the Son, and the Holy Spirit**..."* [2]

The next two pages show two scans of the typed manuscript which this statement comes from. Image 1 shows the page with the actual quote in question and image 2 the first page of the manuscript, which shows Ellen White's own handwriting on the document, making corrections. This shows that Ellen White read the statement in question and approved it how it was typed. Image 3 on page 185 shows Ellen White's original handwriting, where she penned the words of the quote above. Some will point out that she has added "alities" to the word "persons", as proof that she was trying to make a distinction between person and personalities. However the fact that Ellen White's corrections are found on the typed manuscript, and there is not corrections on the quote in question, shows that Ellen White was happy with the typed document.

....
1 For detailed information go to *www.whiteestate.org/issues/The-Trinity.pdf*
2 *Evangelism p. 615, from Special Testimonies, Series B, No. 7, published in 1906.*

-4-

MS 21-'06

the things of earth.   The Father is all the fullness of the Godhead bodily, and is invisible to mortal sight.

Personality of God

The Son is all the fullness of the God-head manifested.
The word of God declares him to be "the express image of his person." "God so loved the world that he gave his only begotten Son,
that whosoever believeth in him should not perish, but have everlasting life." Here is shown the personality of the Father.

The Comforter that Christ promised to send after he
ascended to heaven, is the Spirit in all the fullness of the Godhead, making manifest the power of divine grace to all who receive
and believe in Christ as a personal Savior. There are three living persons of the heavenly trio, in the name of these three great
powers,--the Father, the Son, and the Holy Spirit,--those who
receive Christ by living faith are baptized, and these powers
will co-operate with the obedient subjects of heaven in their efforts to live the new life in Christ.

What is the sinner to do? Believe in Christ. He is
Christ's property, bought with the blood of the Son of God.
Through test and trial the Saviour redeemed human beings from the
slavery of sin. What then must we do to be saved from sin?--
Believe on the Lord Jesus Christ as the sin-pardoning Savior.
He who confesses his sin and humbles his heart will receive forgiveness. Jesus is the sin-pardoning Saviour as well as the only
begotten Son of the infinite God. The pardoned sinner is recon-
ciled to God through Jesus Christ our Deliverer from sin. Keep-
ing in the path of holiness, he is a subject of the grace of God.
There is brought to him full salvation, joy, and peace, and the
true wisdom that comes from God.

Image 1

Scan of the original typed manuscript with the statement regarding the three living persons of the heavenly trio.

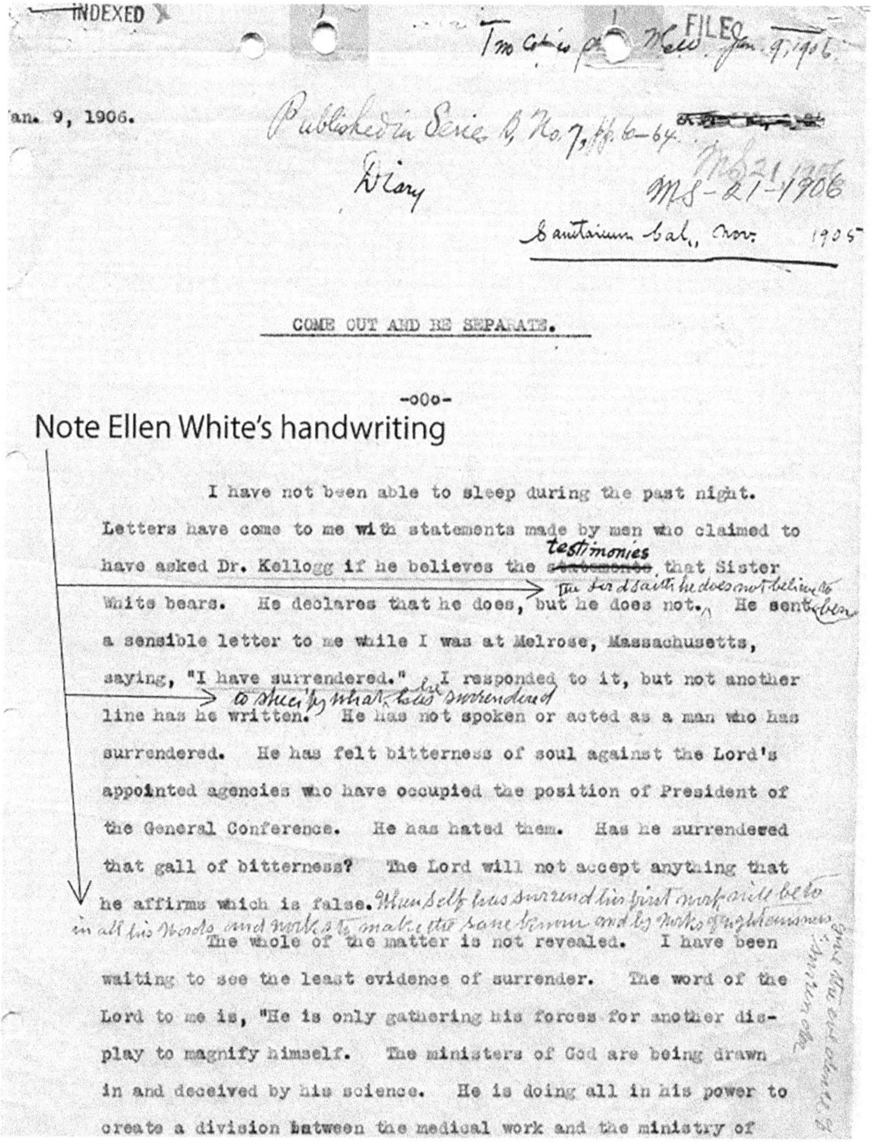

INDEXED

an. 9, 1906.

COME OUT AND BE SEPARATE.

-oOo-

Note Ellen White's handwriting

I have not been able to sleep during the past night.

Letters have come to me with statements made by men who claimed to

have asked Dr. Kellogg if he believes the *testimonies*, that Sister

White bears. He declares that he does, but he does not. He sent

a sensible letter to me while I was at Melrose, Massachusetts,

saying, "I have surrendered." I responded to it, but not another

line has he written. He has not spoken or acted as a man who has

surrendered. He has felt bitterness of soul against the Lord's

appointed agencies who have occupied the position of President of

the General Conference. He has hated them. Has he surrendered

that gall of bitterness? The Lord will not accept anything that

he affirms which is false. The whole of the matter is not revealed. I have been

waiting to see the least evidence of surrender. The word of the

Lord to me is, "He is only gathering his forces for another dis-

play to magnify himself. The ministers of God are being drawn

in and deceived by his science. He is doing all in his power to

create a division between the medical work and the ministry of

Image 2

Scan of page 1 of the original typed manuscript pictured in Image 1.
I have drawn arrows to point to Ellen White's notations in her own
handwriting. This shows clearly that she read the statements before
printing.

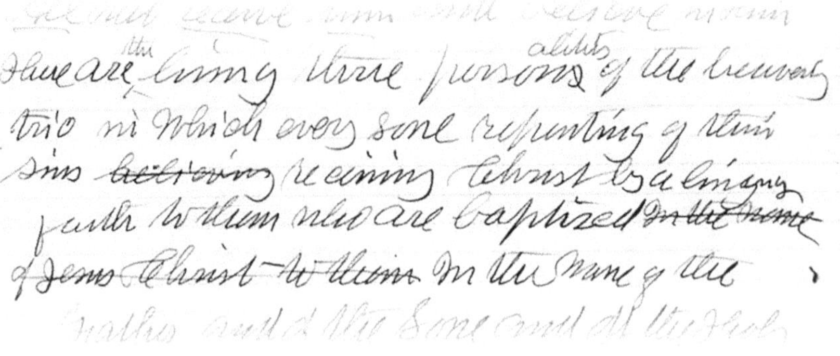
There are the living three persons of the heavenly
trio in which every one repenting of their
sins ~~believing~~ receiving Christ by a living
faith to them who are baptized ~~in the name~~
of ~~Jesus Christ to them~~ in the name of the

Image 3

Furthermore, we find another statement of Ellen White's where she uses the word "persons" also in her own hand writing. Image 4 is a scan of the typed manuscript and Image 5 is the handwritten version. Both are the same. The word "persons" appears in the middle of the first line.

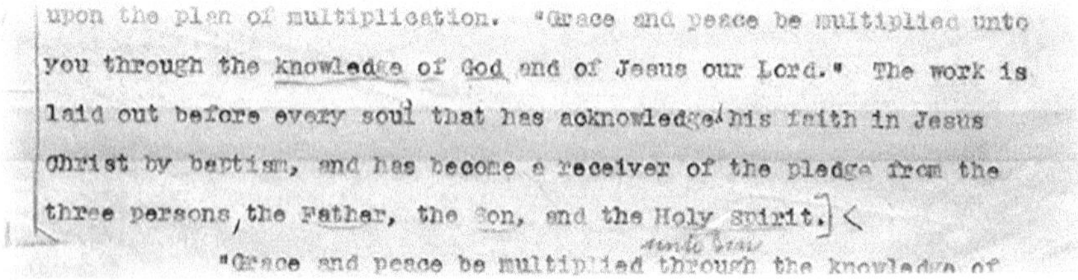
upon the plan of multiplication. "Grace and peace be multiplied unto
you through the knowledge of God and of Jesus our Lord." The work is
laid out before every soul that has acknowledged his faith in Jesus
Christ by baptism, and has become a receiver of the pledge from the
three persons, the Father, the Son, and the Holy Spirit.
"Grace and peace be multiplied unto you through the knowledge of

Image 4

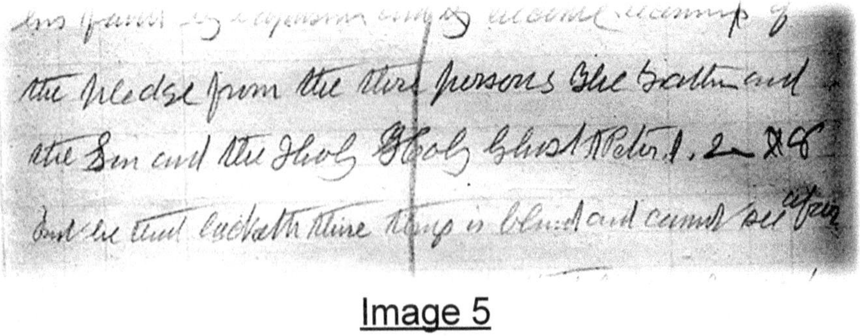
the pledge from the third persons the Father and
the Son and the Holy Holy Ghost II Peter 1. 2 to 8
but he that lacketh these things is blind and cannot see afar

Image 5

"Original, Unborrowed, Underived Life"

*"From Jesus is our life **derived**. In him is life that is **original,—unborrowed, underived life**. In him is the fountain of life. In us there is a streamlet from the fountain of life. Our life is something that we receive, something that the Giver takes back again to himself."* [1]

This statement comes from Letter 309, 1905. Image 6 shows this statement as it was originally typed for printing. Image 7 shows page 6 of Letter 309 which bears Ellen White's signature, showing it to be authentic.

In Jesus is our life derived. In him is life that is original, unborrowed, underived life. In us there is a streamlet from the fountain of life. In him is the fountain of life. Our life is something that we receive, something

Image 6

has gone to prepare for those who will purify their souls by obeying the truth as it is in Jesus. Let every soul who will come after Christ, deny himself, and take up his cross, and follow him. Thus saith the great Teacher.

Love to all the family, *Ellen G. White*

Image 7

The Holy Spirit is a Person"

"The Holy Spirit is a person, for He beareth witness with our spirits that we are the children of God." [2]

....
1   Letter 309, 1905
2   Evangelism p. 616, 617

This statement comes from Manuscript 20, 1906, p. 9. Image 8 shows the typed manuscript with the statement in question. It appears in the second paragraph. The third paragraph states that the Holy Spirit "*has a personality*" and that He is "*a divine person*". Image 9 is the first page of the manuscript. At the top of the page, you will see in Ellen White's own handwriting the words "*I have read this carefully and accept it.*" I have added an arrow to point this out.

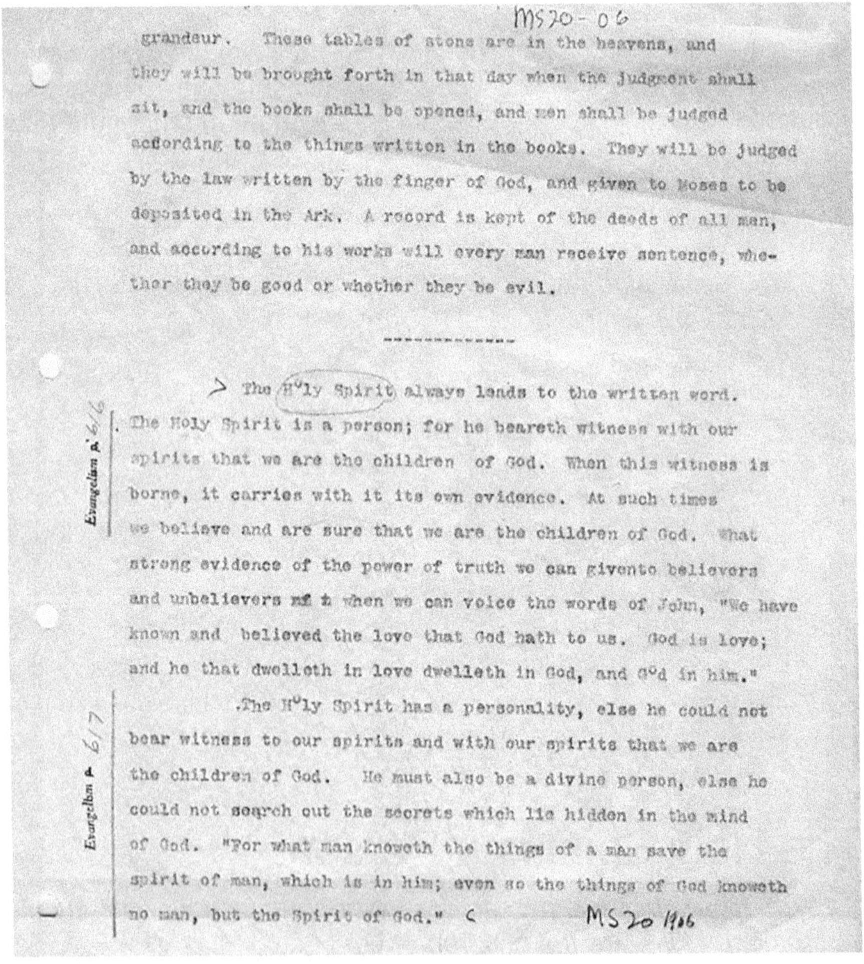

grandeur. These tables of stone are in the heavens, and they will be brought forth in that day when the judgment shall sit, and the books shall be opened, and men shall be judged according to the things written in the books. They will be judged by the law written by the finger of God, and given to Moses to be deposited in the Ark. A record is kept of the deeds of all men, and according to his works will every man receive sentence, whether they be good or whether they be evil.

The H°ly Spirit always leads to the written word. The Holy Spirit is a person; for he beareth witness with our spirits that we are the children of God. When this witness is borne, it carries with it its own evidence. At such times we believe and are sure that we are the children of God. What strong evidence of the power of truth we can give unto believers and unbelievers when we can voice the words of John, "We have known and believed the love that God hath to us. God is love; and he that dwelleth in love dwelleth in God, and G°d in him."

The H°ly Spirit has a personality, else he could not bear witness to our spirits and with our spirits that we are the children of God. He must also be a divine person, else he could not search out the secrets which lie hidden in the mind of God. "For what man knoweth the things of a man save the spirit of man, which is in him; even so the things of God knoweth no man, but the Spirit of God."

Image 8

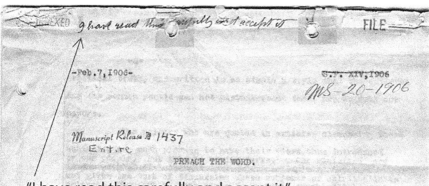

-Feb.7,1906-

U.T. XIV;1906

Manuscript Release # 1437

PREACH THE WORD.

"I have read this carefully and accept it."

[I am instructed that we are not to enter into any controversy over the spiritualistic representations that are fast coming in from every quarter. Farther than this, I am to give those in charge of our papers instruction not to publish in the columns of the Review and Herald, the Signs of the Times, or any other papers published by Seventh-day Adventists, articles attempting to explain these sophistries. We are in danger whenever we discuss the sophistries of the enemy. The publication of articles dealing with these sophistries, is a snare for souls. Let these theories alone, and warn all not to read them. Your explanations will amount to nothing. Let the theories alone. Do not try to show the inconsistency or fallacy of them. Let them alone.

Do not perpetuate evil by talking of these theories in sermons, or by publishing in our papers articles regarding them. The Lord says, Let them be unexplained. Present the affirmative of truth, plainly, clearly, and decidedly. You can not afford to study or combat these false theories. Present the truth, It is written. The time spent in dealing with these fallacies is so much time lost.] Our papers are not published for the purpose of dealing with such subjects. Articles on Bible subjects, full of

Image 9

But if that's not enough, here is the same statement in Ellen White's own handwriting.

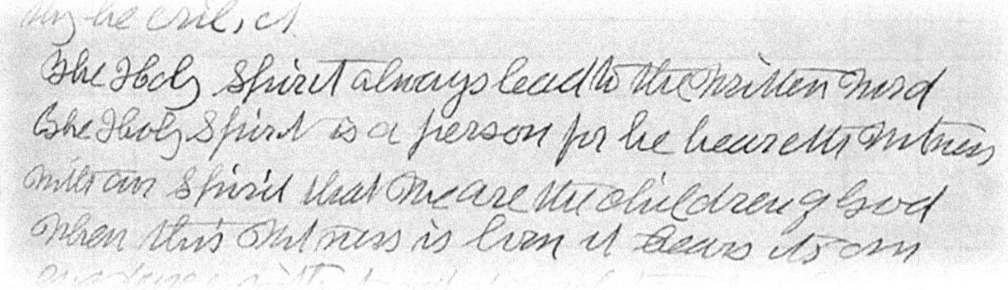
The Holy Spirit always leads to the written word
The Holy Spirit is a person for he beareth witness
with our spirit that we are the children of God
When this witness is born it bears its own

Image 10

"A Distinct Personality"

> *The Holy Spirit is the Comforter, in Christ's name. He personifies Christ, yet is a distinct personality.* [1]

Here is this statement in Ellen White's own handwriting:

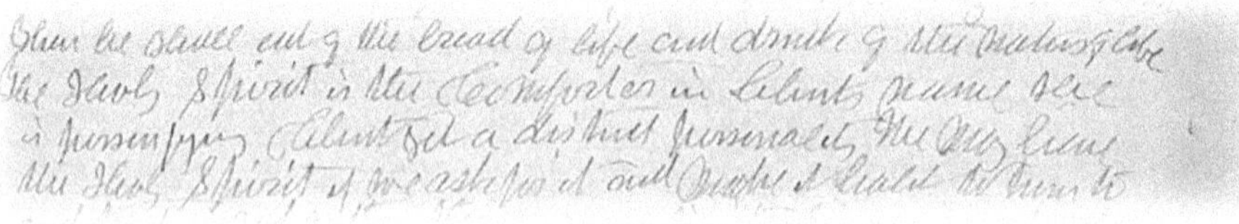
The Holy Spirit is the Comforter in Christ's name He
is personifying Christ yet a distinct personality

Image 11

There are many more such photocopies available. For a more thorough coverage of Ellen White's original statements on the three person Godhead, read Tim Poirier's article from the Ellen White Estate called *"Ellen White's Trinitarian Statements: What Did She Actually Write?"* [2]

I highly recommend Glyn Parfitt's book *"The Trinity: What Has God Revealed?"* It is a nearly exhaustive coverage of the topic of the Godhead.

1 Manuscript 93, 1893, published in Manuscript Releases, vol. 20, pp. 323-325
2 www.whiteestate.org/issues/The-Trinity.pdf

Appendix B

The Trinity in the
Seventh-day Adventist Church
Statement of Beliefs

Anti-trinitarians will point out that the Trinity does not appear in the Seventh-day Adventist church statement of beliefs until 1931. This, they say, is proof that the church apostatized from the truth after Ellen White died. Is this really the case?

The first statement of beliefs was published in 1872, which gives a broad and basic description of the Godhead. You can read it on pages 177-179 of this book. This same statement was republished in the 1889 Year Book. There is no official update to this statement until 1931. In this statement the section on the Godhead reads:

2. That the Godhead, or Trinity, consists of the Eternal Father, a personal, spiritual Being, omnipotent, omnipresent, omniscient, infinite in wisdom and love; the Lord Jesus Christ, the Son of the Eternal Father, through whom all things were created and through whom the salvation of the redeemed hosts will be accomplished; the Holy Spirit, the third person of the Godhead, the great regenerating power in the work of redemption. Matt. 28:19

This is certainly a big change from the 1872 statement. But most people don't realise that this statement was based on an article written by F. M. Wilcox. Wilcox was one of the men handpicked by

Ellen White to be one of the trustees of her writings. This statement of beliefs was published in 1913, two years before Ellen White died, in the Review and Herald. The article is called "The Message for Today". Two paragraphs of the article read as follows:

> *"For the benefit of those who may desire to know more particularly the cardinal features of the faith held by this denomination, we shall state that Seventh-day Adventists believe,—*

> *i. **In the divine Trinity.** **This Trinity** consists of the eternal Father, a personal, spiritual being, omnipotent, omniscient, infinite in power, wisdom, and love; of the Lord Jesus Christ, the Son of the eternal Father, through whom all things were created, and through whom the salvation of the redeemed hosts will be accomplished; **the Holy Spirit, the third person of the Godhead**, the one regenerating agency in the work of redemption."*

Then in 1931 this statement was incorporated into the church's official statement of beliefs. Image 12 on the following page is a scan of the original Review and Herald article. What's most interesting is, this article appears right after one of Ellen White's articles, making it highly likely that Ellen White would have read this article.

So its not true that there were no changes in Adventist thinking regarding the Godhead until after Ellen White died. In fact I believe Ellen White was very instrumental in changing the church's direction in this matter.

name is their watchword, their badge of distinction, their bond of union, the authority for their course of action, and the source of their success. Nothing that does not bear his superscription is to be recognized in his kingdom.

The first disciples went forth preaching the word. They revealed Christ in their lives; and the Lord worked with them, "confirming the word with signs following." These disciples prepared themselves for their work. Before the day of Pentecost they met together, and put away all differences. They were of one accord. They believed Christ's promise that the blessing would be given, and they prayed in faith. They did not ask for a blessing for themselves merely; they were weighted with the burden for the salvation of souls. The gospel was to be carried to the uttermost parts of the earth, and they claimed the endowment of power that Christ had promised. Then it was that the Holy Spirit was poured out, and thousands were converted in a day.

The Saviour longs to manifest his grace and stamp his character on the whole world. It is his purchased possession, and he desires to make men free, and pure, and holy. Though Satan works to hinder this purpose, yet through the blood shed for the world there are triumphs to be achieved that will bring glory to God and the Lamb. Christ will not be satisfied till the victory is complete, and "he shall see of the travail of his soul, and shall be satisfied."

Mrs. E. G. White.

The Message for Today

The Christian church has passed through many crises in its history. Through the ages it has stood as the conservator of the truth of God and the one through whom his messages have been proclaimed to the world. Great movements have engaged her attention. Some of these movements have been specific in their character. To the antediluvians, Noah, the representative of God, preached the message of the coming flood, and under Heaven's direction provided a means of deliverance to all who would accept the proffered salvation. Jonah was sent to warn Nineveh of its impending doom. Through heeding the message which he bore, the inhabitants were saved and the threatened destruction long delayed. When Christ was about to appear among men, chosen messengers from God, the holy angels, John the Baptist, Simeon, Anna, and others proclaimed the glad news of the coming Saviour.

In the order of God other great religious awakenings occurred. The Lord raised up Luther, Melanchthon, Zwingli, and others for the accomplishment of a great work in the Reformation of the sixteenth century. Later a great quickening impulse was given to the cause of Christianity through the Spirit-filled preaching of John and Charles Wesley, George Whitefield, and others.

These movements and messages came for the most part in response to the voice of prophecy. John the Baptist was "the voice of one crying in the wilderness," the voice predicted by Isaiah the prophet. Luther and his colaborers clearly did a

We have reached a period in the history of the church and of the world when, according to the prophecies of the Scripture, the time has come for another great religious awakening. Another message is due the church and the world,—the message of the second coming of the Lord and Saviour to this earth.

This earth's history is soon to close. Fulfilling prophecy and signs — conditions existing in the social, political, industrial, and religious worlds — plainly indicate that a time has been reached when events of a significant, startling, and most stupendous character are about to take place; that the long reign of sin is soon to be cut short; and that the generation now living will witness the appearing of Christ in the clouds of heaven. The message based upon these fulfilling prophecies and signs is now being proclaimed. To the advocacy of this message the people represented by this movement have devoted their lives and their fortunes.

For the benefit of those who may desire to know more particularly the cardinal features of the faith held by this denomination, we shall state that Seventh-day Adventists believe,—

1. In the divine Trinity. This Trinity consists of the eternal Father, a personal, spiritual being, omnipotent, omniscient, infinite in power, wisdom, and love; of the Lord Jesus Christ, the Son of the eternal Father, through whom all things were created, and through whom the salvation of the redeemed hosts will be accomplished; the Holy Spirit, the third person of the Godhead, the one regenerating agency in the work of redemption.

2. That the Holy Scriptures of the Old and New Testaments were given by the inspiration of God, and contain a full revelation of his will to men, and are the only infallible rule of faith and practise.

3. That Jesus Christ, while retaining his divine nature, took upon himself the nature of the human family, lived on this earth as a man, gave his life for the salvation of the race; and that forgiveness and remission of sins, the attainment of spiritual perfection, and the securing of eternal life at last, can be obtained only by faith in his atoning blood and through the redeeming grace which he supplies.

4. That, in fulfilment of the Old Testament types, Jesus, the Son of God, is now "a minister of the sanctuary, and of the true tabernacle, which the Lord pitched, and not man." That, as our great High Priest in this heavenly sanctuary, he presents his own sacrifice before the Father in behalf of sinful men, and to those who will accept it he ministers the needed grace with which they carry on their warfare against sin. Thus he serves as the one Mediator between God and man, rendering both unnecessary and impossible any other system of mediation.

5. That the proper form of baptism is by immersion, and that this ordinance of the Christian church should follow repentance and forgiveness of sins, and that through its celebration faith is shown in the death, burial, and resurrection of Christ.

6. That every soul in order to obtain salvation must experience the new birth. That this comprises an entire transfor-

the recreative agency of the Holy Spirit.

7. That the will of God for his children is comprehended in the law of the ten commandments, and that these are great moral, unchangeable precepts binding upon the children of God in every age of the church.

8. That through the new covenant relationship the Spirit of Christ writes this law upon the heart, and in this way only can its precepts find expression in the life in sincere, faithful obedience.

9. That the fourth commandment of this unchangeable law requires the observance of the seventh-day Sabbath, an institution which was established and ordained in the garden of Eden before man sinned, embosomed in the great law of moral precepts spoken from Mt. Sinai, observed by prophet and priest throughout the old dispensation, kept by Christ and his apostles in the Christian dispensation, and given to mankind in every age to keep alive in their hearts the knowledge of its Author, the Creator of all things.

10. That Christian temperance embraces the proper use of that which is good, and total abstinence from all that is bad. That the liquor traffic, being only evil, should be prohibited by appropriate legislation.

11. That the church and the state occupy different spheres of operation, the former dealing with questions of a religious character, the sphere of the latter pertaining alone to questions of a civil character. The church and the state should therefore be kept forever separate.

12. That the Scriptural means for the support of Christian evangelical work in the earth is by the payment of one tenth of the regular income, and by free-will offerings from the thankful, grateful children of God.

13. That man possesses a nature inherently sinful and dying; that eternal life and immortality come only through the gospel, and are bestowed as the free gift of God by Jesus Christ in the day of final awards.

14. That the time has been reached when the work of the gospel will soon be consummated; when Christ, who now officiates as our great High Priest in the heavens above, will close his ministry and come to this earth to take his children home. That at that time the righteous dead will be raised to meet their Lord, and, together with the righteous living, be changed to glorious immortality.

15. That in the fires of the last day, this earth will be regenerated and cleansed from the effects of the curse; and that in the final conflagration, Satan and all the impenitent will be destroyed. The creation of God will be restored to its pristine beauty and purity, and will forever constitute the abode of the saints of the Lord.

The glad news of the coming kingdom is now going to the world. By tongue and pen, by gospel herald and by printed page, in more than ninety of earth's languages and dialects, the message of the Saviour's soon coming is being carried to the nations of men. The Scriptures of Truth do not reveal the hour nor day nor year when Christ will return, but conditions on every hand proclaim his coming near. He bids us watch and be ready. He bids us give to those in darkness a knowledge of his saving grace. May we prove true to

CPSIA information can be obtained
at www.ICGtesting.com
Printed in the USA
BVHW04s0209260918
528533BV00010B/71/P